MUDDY PEOPLE

MUDDY

A MUSLIM COMING OF AGE

PEOPLE

SARA EL SAYED

GREYSTONE BOOKS
Vancouver/Berkeley/London

First published by Greystone Books in 2022
Originally published in Australia by Black Inc. Books
Copyright © 2021 Sara El Sayed
22 23 24 25 26   5 4 3 2 1

Greystone Books Ltd.
greystonebooks.com

Cataloguing data available from Library and Archives Canada
ISBN 978-1-77164-997-1 (pbk)
ISBN 978-1-77164-998-8 (epub)

Cover design by Alissa Dinallo and Belle Wuthrich
Text design by Belle Wuthrich

Printed and bound in Canada on FSC® certified paper at Friesens.
The FSC® label means that materials used for the product
have been responsibly sourced.

Greystone Books gratefully acknowledges the Musqueam,
Squamish, and Tsleil-Waututh peoples on whose land
our Vancouver head office is located.

Greystone Books thanks the Canada Council for the Arts,
the British Columbia Arts Council, the Province of British Columbia
through the Book Publishing Tax Credit, and the Government
of Canada for supporting our publishing activities.

Canada

FSC
MIX
Paper from
responsible sources
FSC® C016245
www.fsc.org

BRITISH COLUMBIA

BRITISH COLUMBIA
ARTS COUNCIL
An agency of the Province of British Columbia

Canada Council
for the Arts

Conseil des arts
du Canada

To my family—Mama, Baba,
Nana, Aisha and Mohamed.
It is an honour to be part of us.

THE GIRL IN THIS PICTURE is me, just after publishing my first piece of writing, in *Growing Up African in Australia*. I am doing a radio interview and have been asked to provide a headshot. My hair is straightened because I attended a friend's wedding a few days earlier. In this picture my hair is severely damaged. When loose, it sits at approximately six different lengths, and falls out every time I touch it. The state of my hair is due to a combination of harsh chemicals, the wrong hair oil mixed with a too-hot iron, tying it up when it's wet (upon drying, it expands and snaps against the hair tie) and general negligence. I put on a clean white t-shirt and stand in front of my mother's brick house. I think I look okay.

In a few months' time this picture is used again, to accompany an excerpt of a different work of mine, in a magazine. I send the same headshot for everything because I cannot afford to hire a photographer to take a better one. I also cannot afford to straighten my hair again.

When my story runs, I notice that my photo looks a little different. The colour of my skin is lighter. I look again, and I check with friends to make sure that I am not seeing things—that the corners of my mouth have in fact been erased, the size of my lips reduced. I am now pale-faced and pursed-lipped.

At first, I am embarrassed. I hadn't anticipated that the shade of my skin and the size of my lips would be a problem. My hair was the issue, and I'd fixed that. Then I am angry. The kids in school called me *muzzie, mud skin, slave, sand n*gger.* Muzzie, short for Muslim, sounds like *mozzie*—the Aussie word for the parasite that sucks blood. The insect that you swat. I am light-skinned, but back then, it didn't matter. I wasn't white, and that was enough.

Some shout about muddy skin because they think it's funny. Others try to clean you up.

🐾 🐾 🐾

IN A SHED MY MOTHER and I repurposed as a writing space, Gina is curled up on my lap as I sit at my desk. The rain is hammering the roof. Gina is a male cat, but the word for cat in Arabic is feminine, so to us she is Gina.

I'm in Queensland, but in the middle of winter it is cold even in the sun. The small flame of the candle, which I light every day, helps a little. In the winter my hair is drier, my skin paler. I used to relish these months when I felt just a little whiter. But not anymore. When I visit my father on the weekends, he tells me I look ill.

I talk to my father almost every day. The contact is concentrated right now because there's a white boy in the picture, and my father is on guard. He wants me to know the rules. We are Egyptian, after all. We are Muslim, after all. We are not white.

My parents' advice has always been a crucial part of my life. When I say "their advice," I mean them telling me to do things and me doing them. Their rules govern how I live.

Our culture governs how I live. The fact that I am an adult does not change this. There have been many rules over the years, some logical, some not. Sometimes they contradict one another. It means that sometimes things get a little messy. A little muddy.

Writing about my family is not easy, because we are not perfect. I would say we are doing our best, but sometimes we are acting our worst.

On my desk is a stack of books. It's crowned by a wax-spattered copy of *The Family Law* by Benjamin Law—a library copy, so I'm scared to take it back. I borrowed it because I am struggling to write about my family.

I know what people expect when they pick up this book. Stories about racism, about Islamophobia. The name-calling, the ostracising, the bullying. Some of that is in here. But that's not all this book is about. It's about my family, and what we are on the inside too. It's hard to write about family because, as I have explained to my parents, one person's perspective is not the same as another's. My father might say the sky is blue and my mother will say to take an umbrella. The stories we tell don't always match up. That's something that I've had to accept in writing all of this down.

I want my parents to know that this book is told through my eyes: those of a girl growing up and trying to understand. I still have a lot of growing to do. These are versions of my family that have existed to me throughout periods of my life.

I love my parents. They are both good people. They were just not good together.

THESE ARE THE RULES

MAMA LEARNED EARLY ON THAT her daughter was different from her son. Mohamed threw tantrums; Soos stayed quiet if you gave her something sweet. In Arabic, a *soos*, a cavity, is what you get after eating too much sugar. My parents gave me the nickname when I was four. By that time, I had two gold crowns and twice as many holes in my teeth.

In my mouth now, one would struggle to find a tooth not stuffed with a filling. I was never in the habit of maintaining good oral health. We aren't brought up that way; we don't nurture what isn't healthy. When our grass isn't as green as we want, we concrete over it.

Mohamed was difficult from the beginning. Stuck sideways inside my mother, he didn't want to come out.

"It's too much," the delivering doctor said in Arabic, throwing his hands in the air. "He won't budge. I don't know what to do." He left the room to pray and came back smelling like cigarettes. By that time, Mama was screaming and Mohamed was crowning. "By the grace of God," said the doctor.

My father was happy his first child was a boy. They named him Mohamed, like every other baby boy born in Alexandria, Egypt, on that day.

When my grandparents came to see him, the nurse brought the wrong baby.

"That's not my son," said Baba.

His son, of course, was the one with the big nose.

"It was like a hook," Nana tells me, reminiscing about the birth of her first grandchild. She makes a hook shape with her finger, in case words don't do justice to the severity.

"It was big," Mama concurs.

"Huge. So ugly. Like his grandfather's."

"An Arab nose, for sure."

"And he was *green*. All over. Like an alien. Green and a big nose—very unattractive. A truly ugly child."

My father describes my birth as "no problems." The biggest hitch, in fact, was Mohamed asking for squid sandwiches.

"*Soobeyt soobeyt!*" shouted the toddler, standing up in the front seat of our Lada Niva. Baba drove him to the sandwich shop after dropping Mama at the hospital.

I ask Mama about my birth and she describes being knocked out by an anaesthetic, then being shaken awake by doctors telling her to push, then passing out, then waking up to the smell of squid, then seeing the contents of her stomach on the floor.

Mohamed never slept through the night as a baby. Soos never woke up. I didn't even wake during my first *zelzal*, earthquake. I was a newborn, the weight of a bottle of milk. My brother was the weight of a small cow, Mama says.

The zelzal struck in the middle of the night. "Your father picked you up out of your cot and ran downstairs straight-away," says Mama, "and he left the big fat two-year-old to me. Seven flights of stairs. Seven flights of stairs."

❧ ❧ ❧

THE APARTMENT BUILDING WE LIVED in had armed guards out the front, who swung their guns over their shoulders like schoolboys with backpacks. They were there to protect the person who lived on the top floor: a diplomat. Someone from elsewhere who was important enough to kill for.

I was not supposed to talk to the guards, but sometimes they would smile at me when I was with my father. They weren't always around, which somewhat defeated the purpose. But always there, living in what was likely built as a cloakroom, was the porter and his family. I counted seven the last time I got a peek inside. The porter was a friendly old man who treated us like royalty.

He greeted my father, calling him *ustaaz*, professor. My father was not a professor, but this is what people like the porter called people like my father. It was clear to me, even then, that the porter would never be an ustaaz. That title was not made for him.

The porter would stand sentry outside the building when the guards disappeared, sometimes all night. Evening was when people were energised, walking through the streets, kids playing in the park, dripping ice cream down their hands under the watchful eye of their smoking parents. People stayed out even later during Ramadan. One year, when we arrived back home late, the porter greeted my father.

"*Ramadan karim, ya ustaaz*," he said. His voice was croaky from hours spent in silence.

"*Allahu akram*," said my father. The door of the cloakroom was open, and I could hear the family, whispering to one another.

My father thanked the porter for running an errand for him earlier. Baba removed the gold sparkly watch from his wrist and held it out to the porter. "An early Eid gift," he said, in Arabic.

The porter had a hard time accepting, but eventually he took it, looking a little wet-eyed. There was a blotch of ice cream on my father's shirt, from when he had finished my strawberry cone. I wanted to tell him, but I was worried it would ruin the moment.

By morning, a guard would usually be back at his station, giving the porter a chance to sleep. From our seventh-floor balcony, they all looked like toy soldiers. I wasn't scared of them, even with their guns.

A cardboard box on our balcony housed our pet tortoise, Leafy. One day Leafy escaped his box. Being slow, he had plenty of time to think. Even so, he walked right off the edge. His shell shattered when he hit the ground, and the guard who found him threw his body into the bushes of the park opposite the building. Always watching.

From our balcony we could see the entire park. To a child, it was a grand vista; in actuality, it was a circle of turf, lined with hedges twice as tall as a toddler. Pavement ran around the circle, then out diagonally to the corners of the rectangular plot, like the crosshairs of a sniper rifle. But for a long time, it was the biggest place on earth to me.

Baba has a story about a time he took me there. "It was a rainy day, a bad day to go out," he says. "You were walking behind me, and suddenly you started screaming. Screaming and screaming, like you had seen a ghost. You had stopped in front of a puddle of water. You were screaming, 'Sunny! Sunny!' And I said, 'What do you mean, sunny? It's not sunny today.' You keep screaming, 'Sunny! Sunny!' And pointing to the water.

"You were screaming your lungs out. You know, the whole park was looking at us," my father says. "Finally, I got it. You didn't mean *sunny*. You meant *muddy*. You were worried about crossing the water. You got the words confused. You meant one thing and you said something else. The complete opposite. Isn't that funny?"

Wet shoes—that was the problem. I was four, and I was learning how to keep my shoes clean. I had learned at mosque that cleanliness was next to godliness. You had to be clean when you spoke to Allah. Even outside the mosque, clean people got respect—people with neat hair, ironed shirts, pressed trousers and spotless, expensive new shoes. If you didn't have those things, you did not belong in the building. You belonged in the cloakroom.

☙ ☙ ☙

MY BEST FRIEND NOUR'S GRANDMOTHER lived on a street bordering the far side of the park. I could see her piano, which I was never allowed to touch when I visited, through her front window. Nour was as pale as can be, and stupid too. She'd bounce a basketball with two hands, while jumping up and down in time with the ball. Every time I saw that piano through her grandmother's window, I thought about how two-hand-dribble Nour was allowed to play it and I was not. Nour looked sickly, with her pasty skin and black heavy plaits. I didn't want to be like her. I just wanted to touch that piano, and that made me angry. Whenever I visited Nour's house I would make sure Mama brushed my hair back neatly; I checked my clothes didn't have any wrinkles, and I inspected my shoes for muddy spots. But even when I looked perfect, I was never good enough to sit on that piano stool.

❧ ❧ ❧

IN THE BEDROOM I SHARED with Mohamed, the walls were decorated with drawings of Bananas in Pyjamas and a letter that Mohamed had submitted to his Junior Three teacher, titled *I love you Miss Sohad*. A wooden bookshelf bordered one wall. Nana would read to us every night before we went to sleep, the light of our bedroom lamp peeking through the crown of her dyed hair. There was no way there were any natural blondes in our family.

The last book we read together in that room was *Harry Potter and the Philosopher's Stone*. Hermione was my favourite character, because she was a girl and had fuzzy hair, just like me. Nana would pronounce her name how it was spelt: *her-me-own*. When I saw the movie, I realised someone had to be wrong.

Next to the bookshelf sat a toy plastic castle that opened in the middle to reveal petite royal quarters. It came with a tiny princess, no taller than the top half of my finger. She had blonde hair, white skin and no pupils. Her gazeless blue eyes frightened the hell out of me. Princess Shaitan.

One look was all it took before I locked her in the castle and never opened it again.

There was soon to be another little princess in the house. Ear pressed to Mama's belly, I imagined what my new sister would look like. The image of the blonde-haired, blue-eyed, pupil-less princess fixed itself in my mind.

Mama went into labour two weeks before my birthday, in the middle of the night. I awoke to a house with no parents. Nana bundled Mohamed and me into a taxi to take us to school. Our uncle picked us up afterward.

"Have you seen the baby yet?" I asked him.

"No. Not yet," he said. He looked like my father. They had the same pattern baldness.

The car had a sunroof that wasn't letting any sun in. I stood on the seat and stuck my head out. The smell of seawater and garbage water hit me. The streets in Alexandria were plastered with posters of President Mubarak. At the time I thought this meant we loved him—some people even had portraits of him in their homes. Underneath the posters were families sleeping on cardboard. My uncle shouted at me to sit down. Little girls holding their infant sisters begged for money from passers-by.

When we arrived at the hospital, my sister was wearing the Winnie the Pooh outfit I had picked out for her. She smelled of cooling dough, and screamed as I held her. I passed her to Nana and ate the jelly the nurse had left for Mama.

Baba was freaked out by her fingers. "So long and thin," he said. "Creepy."

By the time Aisha was one, she had a head of blonde curls that took everyone by surprise. "Like an alien," Baba said.

Aisha's *sebooua* was the last time I saw all my family and friends in one place. A sebooua is a sort of christening for Muslim babies. So, not a christening at all. A doula came to the house and placed Aisha in a sieve on the floor. She put a large knife next to her, then moved it to the other side, then put the knife on Aisha's little chest. Everyone else walked around the house in a line, a candle in one hand, slipping sugar-coated almonds into their mouths with the other. Nour stepped on the backs of my shoes as we circled the apartment.

I barely recognised anyone. The only sense of warmth was from the candle in my hand and Nour's hot breath on my neck. They all must have been there before, for my sebooua, but I hadn't seen them since. People only show up when there's food.

❧ ❧ ❧

MAMA ALREADY HAD AN AUSTRALIAN passport because she'd lived in Melbourne before. In the 1970s, her father got a job at an architecture firm. Nana remembers the names *Glenferrie* and *Malvern*, and a tram on their doorstep. Nana worked in a library while Mama went to preschool with little girls named Liz.

They stayed until Mama was ten. Then Nana took Mama and fled, back to Alexandria, leaving her husband behind. Nana didn't mind Australia, but there was no place beautiful enough to make her forget the hate she had for her husband.

Mama loved Australia, and promised herself that she would return one day.

"I found it very strange," Baba tells me, "that your mother was so obsessed with Australia. Every year from 1992 to

2001, she would ask me, 'Can we go to Australia now? Can we go to Australia now?' Like a little girl asking to go to the toilet. I don't know why she wanted to go so badly. I kept saying no, I have a business here, we can't go. But it got a bit hard. The business. The money. So I said, 'Okay, fine. Let's go.'"

My parents decided to leave Egypt for good. The economic uncertainty and political unrest that would eventually erupt into a revolution in 2011 was showing its signs.

In 2001, Baba began compiling a binder of all the suburbs in Brisbane—comparing house prices, schools, jobs. He spent weeks on the computer researching.

Since Mama was already a citizen, her children could become Australians too. But Baba had to get a visa.

"Are you sick?" I asked as he prepared to see a physician. We didn't visit doctors in my family, because Mama was a doctor. We only had to show Mama our cut or the colour of our poo—she'd figure out what to do. Baba seeing someone else was odd.

"No. But I have to get checked before they let us go."

"Why, if you aren't sick?"

"These are the rules," he said.

Years later, Baba tells me what the physician said that day. "There was a shadow behind my heart," he says. "He didn't know what it was. He just saw a shadow there. But he let me go. To him, I was healthy." Baba places both his hands on his chest. "You know, when I was young and I played with my friends, I always had a problem with breathing. I couldn't run for so long. And I think—I know—it was the shadow. If the doctor had known at that time. If he had known what it was, maybe he would have tried to treat it. Maybe it couldn't have been treated. Either way, we wouldn't have come here. We would've stayed in Egypt. I would be alive or dead. But I would be alive or dead there—not here. The shadow has been behind my heart for a very long time. Allah put it there a very long time ago."

In his bedroom, twelve years after his first doctor's visit since marrying my mother, Baba's lymph nodes swell and press against the nerves in his back, his abdomen and behind his heart, and he falls to his knees.

❧ ❧ ❧

THERE WAS A ROOM IN our Alexandria flat with couches no one was allowed to sit on. A carpet no one was allowed to walk on. No muddy footprints. No feet at all.

Most families I knew had this. A salon. A façade for friends. A gold-framed picture of my parents on their wedding day hung on the wall. It was near the balcony, and in the afternoons the light would catch on the frame, and on the edges of the furniture.

When we moved, we took at least one thing from every room. From the living room, videotapes of Teletubbies and family celebrations. From the kitchen, plums to eat on the way to the airport, which ended up giving us all diarrhea. From Mohamed's and my bedroom, *Harry Potter and the Philosopher's Stone*. From my parents' room, the Qur'an. But we did not take a thing from the salon—from that sunny room. That room was to be preserved as it was at all costs.

My parents are still there, hanging on the wall.

BABA

I WANT TO TALK ABOUT my father. I'm sunk in the plastic chair next to him, and he is in a much nicer chair, surrounded by nurses who are growing frustrated. They are prodding his arms with a needle, trying to find a vein. They are frustrated because my father is frustrated, and he can be coarse when this happens. He asks them to draw the curtain around him. I can see he is angry. The other chemo patients in their chairs are pretending not to look. A nurse pulls a curtain around the chair, and my father starts to cry. Angry tears flick from his lips.

He says he wants to go home, but it's 2014 and home for him is now 3000 kilometres away, in Katherine, Northern Territory. He is here, in Queensland, only for this. He says there is no point if they can't find a vein, and the nurses almost agree. They leave, telling him they will be back later to try again. My father wipes his tears on his sleeve.

"Do you want anything?" I ask him.

"Cappuccino," he says. His voice raises when he says no sugar, because he's been burned by me before. He points to his bag. I take his wallet and pull out the tip of a twenty-dollar note. He nods and I stuff it in my pocket.

The Gold Coast hospital has won design awards. The glass walls exposing the arriving maxi taxis and shuttle buses remind me of an airport. The central staircase is panelled with artwork—stencilled silhouettes of trees and blades of grass in aqua, white and black. One image stands out from the rest. It is a burst of red that spans across three white panels. A thick branch holds several thin branches, and those branches hold many thinner. On the ends of some are swollen fruits—pears or apples. They are the same shade of red as the branches. The picture is how my father describes his lymphoma.

The café is called Doctors Orders, which was cute at first. I ask for a hot chocolate, because coffee gives me heart palpitations, and a large cappuccino with no sugar. I watch the barista as he dusts cocoa on the cappuccino. I know that if my father was here he would say, *Hey, I said no sugar. Coco is sugar.* I let it go. He is stuck in the chair, which means he can only argue with people who come to him.

I return to the chemo ward and hand him the takeaway cup. I watch him as he sips it. It is too hot, he says. Burning.

❧ ❧ ❧ RULE NO. 1 ❧ ❧ ❧
DON'T TOUCH ALCOHOL

AUSTRALIA WAS CLOSED ON SUNDAYS. A ghost country. The streets were empty of cars, garbage and people. We had sixteen suitcases, each tagged with red, white and blue ribbons that aunties had plaited for us. I looked out the window of the maxi taxi as we drove away from the airport after our twenty-four-hour journey and did not see a single thing move, aside from the road. We had entered a still image. A billboard of Australia. We were in The Down Under.

Our guardian, the taxi driver, had a neat beard like Baba and wore a turban. Baba had been bald since at least his wedding photos. The driver and Baba spoke back and forth, neither understanding the other's accent. But both were laughing as if they understood something much more important. Or, more likely, nothing at all.

It was January 2002, and it was hot. The air conditioning hardly reached the back seat. Nana, who was sitting in the middle row of the taxi next to Mama and Aisha, turned to Mohamed and me.

"Remember," she said, "Australia is where kangaroos live. Tell me if you see one."

"I saw one! I saw one!" said Mohamed, his fat hand pressed against the window, his breath fogging up the glass. "It was hopping near the road!"

He was a liar. I looked for the whole trip and didn't see a single one.

❧ ❧ ❧

WHEN WE FIRST ARRIVED IN Morningside, named for the nineteenth-century sunrises hitting the hills, Baba booked two rooms at the Colmslie Hotel, named for the house of a colonial aristocrat who delighted in horseflesh. In the hotel, Mohamed and I were in one room with Nana; Aisha was in the other with Mama and Baba.

Across the road was a small shopping complex, of the blandest colours and geometry the 1960s had offered. The place echoed with the emptiness of absent churchgoers and late sleepers. The lights in the supermarket were off. A mat sat at the door of the butcher, imprinted with a deceptive *welcome*. We were still in our clothes from the plane, Aisha's spittle encrusting Mama's t-shirt. "Does no one eat on Sunday?" Mama said.

A produce store had its roller doors up, and there was a man inside, sweeping the floor. Baba approached him.

"Hello. You are open." He said this as a question, but it sounded more like a command.

"No," said the man. "This is closed. I'm the cleaner."

"But you are open," said Baba.

"No, I don't work here. I am the cleaner of the complex."

"But you are working here. I need to buy food for my kids."

"I can't help you, sorry."

My father didn't understand. "I need food!"

"Fine," the startled man said. "Take it."

Baba started gathering food in a basket. He took it up to the counter. "I pay here?"

"No. No one is here to take your money."

"But you are here. I have to pay."

"I don't work here!"

"I have to pay. I am not a thief."

"Fine. Give me ten bucks."

Next stop was a nearby petrol station, whose counter housed a lady clad in hi-vis. He bought some bread, milk and five semi-frozen meat pies.

"What time ... do you go home today?" he asked the lady in his halting English.

She looked disturbed. "Excuse me? I'm not telling you that," she said.

"No, no." Baba was embarrassed. "What time do you stop work here?"

"Oh. Do you mean what time do we close?"

"Yes. Sorry."

"Four pm."

"Okay. Sorry." He watched her scan the meat pies one by one. "Are these beef?"

"I think so," she said.

"Are they halal?"

The lady looked at him, confused.

He coughed and rephrased. "How were they made?"

"Do you mean how do you cook them? You just warm them in the oven."

DON'T TOUCH ALCOHOL | 19

"We have no oven. We are at Colmslie." He pointed out the window.

"Oh. A microwave will do."

The hotel held two appliances we had never used before. One: a toaster. Mohamed and I were fascinated and kept making toast. We didn't have square bread in Egypt, we had *shami*—a round flat loaf, which people in Australia like to call pita bread, or Lebanese bread, or wraps. We'd toast shami in the oven, or on a naked flame on the stovetop. I'd watch Mama flip the bread over with her fingers, not feeling the flame. But Australians didn't use stoves with flames, Baba said. They used stoves made of plastic and electricity. Australians only cooked with fire for fun, when they went camping and pretended to live like cavemen. They didn't wash their assholes, either. No one owned a bidet. We each had four showers a day in the Colmslie.

Two: a microwave. We had never used a microwave before—and Baba wasn't about to start the day we arrived in a foreign country. When he got back from the petrol station, he bit into the cold pie. He spat it out. "Eh da? Yuck." But he ate the rest of it so as not to waste food.

❦ ❦ ❦

BACK IN EGYPT, BABA WAS an engineer and an architect. In Australia, he was nothing. He started taking cash jobs, laying bricks.

"I am an educated man," Baba said, "but for my family I will do anything." The difficulty manifested physically. In his back, when he lifted loads. In his fingers, which calloused and formed a tough skin. In his mouth, as he tried to connect.

"Can I get you anything while I'm at the shop?" he asked the other workmen on break. He thought fetching their lunch would make him some friends.

"Just a pie and a ginger beer for me, thanks, mate," said one, a greasy-looking man in his twenties.

"Sorry, mate," Baba said, uneasy. "I can't buy those sort of things."

"Huh?"

"Beer things. It's against my god." He pointed to the sky. Baba took his religion very seriously. He never drank alcohol. Was never in the vicinity of alcohol if he could help it.

"No mate, it's not beer. It's ginger beer. No alcohol," said the guy, laughing.

"I don't do this. I won't buy it."

"It's just a soft drink."

"I won't fall for a trick, mate. Beer is beer. I know what beer is, mate. I can buy something else."

Despite his difficulties in making friends, it wasn't long before Baba found a position as a foreman. He soon had a cooler for a lunchbox and a hard hat without a scratch on it. He was working on a site in Hamilton—a skyrise apartment building near the wharf. Once it was finished, it filled with occupants almost immediately. Baba was immensely proud of himself. They started work on a second building to face the first. By then, the group of tradies he worked with had earned themselves a reputation with Baba.

"Every time a lady or a girl walks past the site, they go crazy," he said. "The boys point and stare, like monkeys. I don't understand this. Because some of them have beautiful wives and girlfriends who come by and drop off their lunch.

Then they go and do this staring thing. It's not good. It makes the new residents unhappy."

One lady complained to Baba's boss. She said their ogling was making her uncomfortable. His boss came to the site and handed Baba an envelope.

"Don't look inside, but take this up to the lady on the fifth floor," he said.

"Why can't I look?" said Baba.

"Because if you look, I know you won't want to take it to her."

Baba looked inside. It was a Beer, Wine and Spirits voucher. "I don't want to be involved in alcohol," said Baba.

"It's a gift," said his boss, "a peace offering. To make her happy. From me to her. Not from you. You're just delivering it. Can you do that for me?"

Reluctantly, Baba made his way up to the fifth floor. He knocked on the door and was greeted by a young woman who looked like she was on her way to the gym.

"Hello. Peter sent me to make you happy," said Baba.

The woman turned red. "I've had enough of this crap. Fuck off," she said, and shut the door in his face.

Baba was embarrassed. He gave the envelope back to his boss and resolved never to touch anything to do with alcohol again.

We moved from the Colmslie to a modest three-bedroom, with a landlord who lived next door. The house was beneath a flight path, and the whirr of planes, with time, would come to remind us of the ocean.

The landlord was a nice man with two kids and a new wife. He would peek over the fence every time we were in the yard and ask us what we were doing, in a friendly way. We didn't meet our neighbours on the other side at first. We could hear and smell their chickens, which strutted around their garden, and we could see the Australian flag that flew from the thick pole that sprouted in it.

During our first week in that house, I watched an episode of *Hi-5* where Kellie uncovered a time capsule she had supposedly buried when she was a little girl. I decided that I, too, would make a time capsule. As we had just moved from across the world, we didn't have many things we were willing to part with. But I was determined to capture our family as we were—a new start, in a new house, in a new country.

In the dining room, my mother's arms were stuck to the plastic gingham-patterned tablecloth, which was covered with newspapers, and the newspapers covered in highlighter. Mama's latest rejection was from the supermarket, where she had applied to be a cashier.

"Do you have anything I can put in our time capsule?" I asked her. She didn't answer. I asked again. "Do you have anything?"

"I'm busy, Soos," she said, her eyes reflecting the vacancies. "Anything?"

She reached across the table and grabbed a wad of junk mail. "Here," she said.

I thought of a place that was full of things no one would miss: the rubbish bin. I dug through and found an empty yoghurt tub. I washed it out and stuffed it in with the junk mail. Also in the bin was a box with the words *rum balls* written in cursive, still full.

If there was one thing Baba hated, it was waste. It was haram to waste food. Since that cold pie from the petrol station, I'd seen him spit out food only once—when the landlord gifted him that box of rum balls on moving day. He put a ball in his mouth and read the box, saw the word *rum*, spat it out, rubbed his tongue with a baby wipe and rushed to the bathroom to gargle. He did this with the same energy one might lick the salt off the back of their hand, down a shot and suck a lemon.

I took two rum balls out of the box and put them in my time capsule.

The ground in the yard was hard and dry, so I dug a hole in the loose bark that sat at the base of the tree on the nature strip. The time capsule was a box of us. This is the story it told: we liked yoghurt, because the yoghurt tub was licked clean; we received junk mail, because we finally had a mailbox; and we never, ever ate rum balls, because we were Muslim.

"Excuse me," called a voice from behind. The lady from next door, the chickens-and-flagpole side. She was wearing horse-riding boots, and her hair was coiffed in a ponytail that pulled her forehead taut. She looked like she would smell overwhelmingly perfumed. She must have been watching me burying the capsule, but had kept her distance. When she spoke, she sounded polite: "Your rubbish doesn't belong on our street."

BABA

ONLY ONE NURSE COMES BACK to talk to my father. She is
Māori—I can tell by her accent and the tattoo on her chin.
When Mohamed got a tattoo of the Sphinx on his arm, my
father said he would go to hell, then kissed him on his head
and bought him lunch. I wait for my father to say something
about the nurse's tattoo, but she speaks first.

"What do we have here?" she says, looking him in the eye.
She is holding a heat pad in her hand. "I'm told your veins
have been playing hide and seek."

"I'm so tired," my father says. "I'm so sick of it. I want to go."

She smiles at him and places the heat pad on his arm. "Hold
it there. Two minutes," she says, before walking out again.

My father gets sweaty when he is stressed. He says he's
been waking in the middle of the night with a drenched pil-
lowcase. He says the doctor tells him it's due to the cancer.
He removes his cap, pulls a handkerchief out of his pocket
with his free hand and wipes his bald head, plus the very
little grey he has on the sides. He leaves the handkerchief
on his head and replaces his cap.

I've broken the unused coffee stirrer in two; it's splin-
tered in my hand. When the nurse pulls back the curtain, I

register the stillness of the trees outside. The ward smells of alcohol wipes and sugar. The woman sitting across from my father is eating malt sticks.

Her name is Rita, the Māori nurse. It is on the ID card hanging from her neck. Rita takes the heat pad off my father's punctured arm. He starts praying as she takes a needle and slides it in. It goes in easy, like he's made of tapioca. He flinches, but it's only out of habit.

"Like magic," says Rita. "All it takes is a little warmth and a little time."

My father looks at the line in his arm and the sack of clear liquid. To the untrained eye, it could be water. But water gives life, and this stuff does opposite, despite its intentions.

My father smiles. "Yes," he says, "you are magic."

❦ ❦ ❦ RULE NO. 2 ❦ ❦ ❦

GOOD GIRLS DON'T WEAR BIKINIS

I STOOD IN FRONT OF the bathroom mirror after my shower with nothing but a towel on my head. Baring all but my hair. *This is what I'd look like if I wore hijab*, I thought. I didn't look bad. The towel framed my face well, and my nose sat nicely in the middle. At seven years old, it hadn't reached its full potential, size-wise. It was an at-risk nose, but not as bad as Mohamed's. Not yet. I twisted the towel up in a turban, like a sister who wears hijab for fashion. Pious and chic. I could pull it off if I wanted to. But here is the thing: I didn't want to wear hijab. And Mama didn't want to, and Nana didn't want to either. We had flown to Brisbane four months after 9/11, and Baba told people at the mosque that Mama didn't wear hijab because the times were sensitive and our names had given us enough trouble at the airport.

This was half true. But the full truth is this: some people don't wear hijab, for no reason other than they just don't want to.

It's hard to know who your people are; walking around with a hijabi wife or daughter makes it easier. I had watched

Baba at the Underwood Shopping Centre—thirty minutes' drive from where we lived, but the only place in Brisbane with a halal butcher—nod at every man who had a hijabi woman by his side. A strong nod, and a smile, as if to say, *just so you know, I'm one of you too.* Despite the exposed curly hair on the girl beside him. We made it harder for Baba to connect with his people. We knew this, and if we really wanted to, we could have made it easier. But I didn't, and neither did Mama.

My mother was engaged to another man before marrying my father. When I ask her about it, she says, "He was handsome. A dentist. A very handsome dentist."

Maybe if Mama had married a very handsome dentist instead of Baba, I would have had better oral health, and my nickname would not be Soos.

"Then why didn't you marry him?"

"He wanted me to wear hijab. And I didn't want to."

Nana interjects. "You know, he called me and said, 'I insist your daughter wear a scarf or I won't marry her.' And I said, 'I insist you stick a shoe up your arsehole.' *Ibn el kelb.*" Son of a dog.

"He also had a lisp I couldn't stand," says Mama.

"Soos, whatever you do, do not marry an Egyptian man," says Nana. But Baba is an Egyptian man, and he didn't force Mama to do anything.

❧ ❧ ❧

THE FIRST DAY OF SCHOOL was an itchy type of hot. Mama dropped Mohamed and me at the gate with little more than "*Yalla*, see you later." Aisha had been bawling in the back seat and wouldn't let go of my new school hat, so I had to leave it with her. The silhouette of the wide brim mocked me as they drove away, and I swear she raised her tiny, two-year-old hand up to the glass and flipped me off. She is the youngest, and she gets what she wants.

Morningside Primary was different from our school in Alexandria. That was a tall structure hard to distinguish from an office building. Morningside, in comparison, was flat. It was not one building but multiple wooden-clad blocks on stilts, spread liberally across land, as if the people who built it were trying to claim as much space as they could.

Mohamed and I walked up the steps to reception, where a lady with long nails sat behind an expansive counter.

"Hello," she said.

"It's our first day here and we don't know where to go," said Mohamed.

"Oh. Is your parent with you?"

"No," said Mohamed.

"What's your name?"

"Mohamed."

The lady typed slowly into the computer. She stared at the screen for a long time.

"*M-O-H-A-M-E-D*," he spelt.

We were told to wait in reception. I watched as students came in late and were signed in by their parents and kissed goodbye as they ran out the door, knowing exactly where to go, knowing exactly who was waiting for them in their classrooms.

A blond boy with dirty shoes entered. He spoke to the office lady, who pointed at Mohamed.

"Wait," I said, holding onto my brother's bag strap as he stood up. "Don't leave me."

He pulled my hand away. "Don't be a baby," he said, and left with the boy.

The office was silent but for the tapping of the keyboard from behind the desk. I read the names of past students on the boards mounted on the walls behind the receptionist. They were embossed in gold and sparkled with reputation. None of them read anything like *M-O-H-A-M-E-D*.

Finally, the door opened, and in came a girl with pink-and-white sneakers. She looked like Lisa from *The Saddle Club*. Not in the way that people told me I looked like Carole just because I was brown; this girl really looked like Lisa. A charm dangled from the loop of her shoelace. From afar it looked like a question mark, but as she got closer, I could see it was half a heart. She had a friend, somewhere, with the other half.

"I have to take you to class," she said. Her heavy Australian accent made each word peel off thin and long, like string cheese. I got up, keeping my eyes on her shoelace.

We walked across a courtyard, up some wooden stairs, and along what I would call a balcony but was told was a ver-an-dah. Along the verandah sat wooden shelves filled with a variety of schoolbags, varying degrees of filth on the base of each. Someone had left their zip open, and a pink plastic lunchbox poked out like a baboon's bottom. In my backpack was a plastic bag with a shami roll in it.

The classroom was big, with desks set up in groups. Students were sitting in a circle on the blue-grey carpet, listening to the teacher. The girl with the shoelace charm joined the circle.

"Hello," said the teacher. He was wearing a black-and-red striped t-shirt and glasses that were too big for his face.

His hair was blond and floppy, falling across his eyes. Something about him made him look untrustworthy. I decided he reminded me of the Hamburglar. "Welcome," he said. "My name is Mr. R. Lilly, will you scooch over, please? Make some room." I figured Lilly was the girl with the charm on her shoe, and that "scooch" meant "move your arse."

"There's no room," said Lilly.

"Can everyone scooch back and make the circle bigger?" said Mr. R. It made me nervous, the way he kept asking the students to do things instead of ordering them. As if they could say no and that would be that: I wouldn't be allowed in. But the circle thankfully expanded. The opening that presented itself was still a bit too small, so I sat behind the circle.

"We were just seeing how many Australian foods we can name. Can you think of any?" said Mr. R.

I thought back to what we'd eaten at home the night before. "Pizza," I said.

"That's not Australian, that's Italian," said a whiny-sounding girl on the other side of the circle. Some kids laughed.

"That's all right," said Mr. R. "Can you give it another go?"

"Square bread," I said.

Mr. R looked at me for a moment. I knew he thought I was dumb. 'That's all right,' he said again. *That's all right* clearly meant *you're wrong*. "Does anyone else want to have a go?"

"Vegemite," said the whiny girl.

"Good!" said Mr. R.

"Pavlova," said a boy.

"Excellent!"

"Sausage sizzle," said another boy.

"Good one!"

Mr. R pulled me aside once he'd settled the rest of the class at their desks with their books. He came close, like he was trying to prove he wasn't afraid of me. His skin was red and acne-ridden. It looked like it needed a wash and maybe some cream.

"Did you bring colouring pencils with you today?"

I shook my head. I did bring pencils, but they weren't the same brand as everyone else's. They lacked the right shiny gold logo.

"You can borrow these." He handed me a cup of pencils. Half of them were broken, and there was no sharpener. "If you're having trouble in class today, just let me know, okay?"

"Okay."

"And before I forget," he pulled a blue piece of paper out of his desk drawer, "take this home to your mum. It's a permission slip for the swimming carnival next week. Do you think you'll be all right to swim? Is that something you can do?"

I nodded.

"Well, that's all good, then."

❧ ❧ ❧

I ARRIVED ON THE DAY of the swimming carnival with my brand-new blue Speedo one-piece with fluoro-green trimming beneath my uniform. I was no stranger to the water—Nana had me in swimming lessons by the time I was two. Mohamed was a pretty good swimmer too: his nose made for an effective keel. Our school in Egypt didn't have a pool, so this felt like a privilege.

The whole school entered the pool complex through the one gate, bottlenecking at the narrow passage. Near the entrance was a concrete canteen displaying an illustration of a flying fish, the words *Morningside Flyers* curving with the fish's trajectory. Kids filed into the grandstand. Mohamed sat among the older boys in the higher seats, and I sat next to Lilly and her friends, closer to the edge of the pool. They were all wearing identical bikinis, in different shades of pink. I imagined their mothers, who each looked like older versions of their daughters, on group shopping dates, buying the same costume in order for their girls to look perfectly cute, a set of dolls.

The marshals blew their whistles and called for different groups of students to line up for their races. Every kid wore a yellow swimming cap plastered with the image of the flying fish, which accentuated how alien in shape their head was. I didn't have a cap. Mohamed's fuzzy head in the sea of yellow baldies calmed my nerves a little. He didn't have one either.

Grade One breaststroke was on first. For a country that was meant to be all about beaches, the kids were rubbish swimmers. They thrashed around in the water; it was a miracle no one drowned.

"I need to go to the toilet," Lilly announced. "Come with us."

"I think our race will be soon," I said.

"If I don't go, I will pee in the pool," she said. "Come on."

I knew it was crass to talk about going to the bathroom, but I rather liked the way she said things straight. She didn't care about being rude.

The girls got up and followed Lilly, and I didn't want to sit alone. The toilets, wall-to-floor concrete, were at the back of the changing rooms. I waited outside the stalls for Lilly and her friends.

"Aren't you going to go?" said Lilly, washing her hands in the sink.

"No." A marshal shot a blank to start the last Grade One race. "It's our grade's turn soon."

She pressed the empty soap dispenser over and over. Nothing came out, but she didn't seem to notice. "If you're not going to go to the toilet, then why did you come with us?"

It was hard to think of an answer other than, "You asked me."

"No, I didn't," she said. "Why would I ask you to come to the toilet with me?"

"I don't know."

"Did you come to perv on us?" She flicked her hands dry.

I didn't know what perv meant, but by the way she said it, I assumed it was bad. I went into the stall, took off my uniform and pulled down my one-piece. I held it under my knees so it didn't touch the piss-encrusted floor and tried to go, but nothing came.

A voice on the megaphone called for the Grade Twos.

"Hey!" said Lilly.

"I'm coming. Sorry. You can go without me," I said. My costume had twisted on itself. I tugged at it, pulling it awkwardly over my knees. It hugged my thighs tight and wouldn't go up any further.

"I have a question," said Lilly. I heard the girls start sniggering. I could see the charm of Lilly's shoelace underneath the door, dangling against her pink-and-white sneaker. It looked like a question mark again. I looked up and met her eye through the gap in the door.

"Why are your nipples so big?" she said.

The girls burst out laughing.

I crossed my arms over my chest, and my one-piece fell around my ankles, onto the wet floor. I didn't know the answer. "I have an infection," I said. It was the first thing that came to mind. I'd heard Mama talk about infections before. I'd seen pictures of embarrassing marks on skin in her textbooks.

"What? Ew," said Lilly.

Finally, I peed. Just a drop. It dribbled down my leg and fell into the still-knotted crotch of my Speedo.

It was the first time anyone had seen me naked, apart from Nana and Mama when I was a baby. It was the first time I understood what it meant to be violated. And it was the first time I developed a deep, seething hatred for a white girl. In that moment, I hated Lilly. Not because she had humiliated me, but because whatever she had under her suit was already understood as better than what I was stuck with. Pink and dainty, just like her bikini. It took her pointing it out for me to realise that my body was different. A joke.

The girls left the bathroom, and I missed my race. I spent the rest of the day in the grandstand and went home with my bathing suit dry in all but one spot.

"I need a bikini," I said to Mama in the car.

"You don't *need* a bikini. You don't *need* anything," she said.

"Yes, I do. It's the rule at school. I have to have a bikini."

"Well, this is our rule: no bikinis."

"I wouldn't have to take off all of my clothes if I wore a bikini."

"Take off all your clothes? Why are you taking off your clothes?"

"In the changing rooms."

"Keep your clothes on. Keep your maillot on. Do not take anything off."

"But I needed to pee."

"Keep it on. Just move the bit to the side."

"What if I need to poo?"

"*Iskooti ba-aa*. Be quiet."

"Just poo your pants," said Mohamed from the back seat.

"Why can't I have a bikini?" I said.

Mama didn't answer.

"It's not fair. You're forcing me to show my nipples to everyone like a perv."

Mama pulled over to the side of the road. I choked a little as my seatbelt pulled taut. "You are a rude girl," she said, without looking at me. We sat in silence for a while. I could tell Mama knew what *perv* meant. When she was angry, the protruding veins in her legs spread to her forehead.

"You are a very rude girl. I didn't bring you here to learn to speak like this." She looked at me, and I looked away. "You need to get your head out of the rubbish. We are not here forever." She said *here* like she meant more than *Australia*. "You need to follow the rules. When I tell you to do something, you do it. When I tell you you can't do something, you can't do it. People can be dirty. I don't care what these people do. But you are not to be dirty. Do you understand?"

"Can we go now?" said Mohamed.

That afternoon, I got out of the shower and stood in front of the mirror with a towel on my head, my dry Speedo curled up in the corner. *This is what I'd look like if I wore hijab. If I were a modest girl. If I weren't a perv.* This girl would not show her nipples to strangers. This girl would not say *nipple* in front of her mother. This girl would listen and do as she's told.

I looked at my chest and saw it for how ugly it was. I pulled the towel off my head and wrapped it around my body, covering my torso.

This girl would not be dirty.

MAMA

THIS IS HOW A CONVERSATION between my mother and her mother starts. My mother will be in the kitchen, and will call, *do you want tea?* Nana, who is in the living room, will not answer. My mother will call again, *do you want tea?* Nana will not answer. My mother will call one more time, *do you want tea?* And Nana will say, *are you talking to me?* My mother has done this for as long as I can remember.

"Have you been talking to your dad?" I ask her.

"How do you know?" she says.

"You've been emailing him."

"He emails me."

"And I saw you got a text from 'Pa'."

"Why are you looking at my phone?"

"Do you reply?"

"Sometimes."

She stirs sweetener into her cup. The kitchen in the home we live in now is not the same as it used to be. There are things that she waited until Baba left to change. She has replaced the countertop—what was once a sweaty brown cork is now white marble. There is a new fridge that dispenses water, and the gaps in the stairs have been boarded up, the empty space beneath them made into a walk-in pantry.

We sit at the dining table. Her laptop is open—she is looking at houses on a real estate website. She does this a lot.

"I hate this house," she says. "I always did."

In this house, we've been robbed three times. The first time, they cut a hole in the front-window flyscreen, reached through and took my mother's handbag, which was sitting on the table nearby. Later that evening a girl, drunk, and her friend, drunker, came to the door. They'd found a wallet—licence, various cards and a small photograph of my grandfather strewn down the footpath. The drunk girl gingerly offered the stuff back to my mother. The cash and credit cards were missing.

The second time, they stole Mohamed's bike. He parked it in the afternoon, and it was gone in the morning. We suspected the neighbours. They kept odd things in their yard, like rusty chains and what looked like the bench from the dog park.

The third time, someone jumped into our backyard, unscrewed the flyscreen from the bedroom window, took it off the frame and stole my mother's handbag off her bed. In the morning we found the empty bag, which had been flung into the hedge outside our house. This was all when that bedroom was still my parents' and not just my mother's.

She called the police after the first theft, but not for the second two. She thinks police only waste time.

She shows me the shortlist of houses, none of which she will ever buy. She's trying to please everyone. Aisha will need to be near her school—she is in Grade Nine and won't get her licence for another couple of years, at least. Mohamed will need a room big enough for his drum kit. Nana would like a place right on the beach, like at home, in Agami; she wants a replica of the house she stays in when she goes back to Egypt each year.

Nana is missing her house even though she's only just got back from her annual trip. Each time she returns to Egypt, she makes sure to visit our old flat in Alexandria, which is only thirty minutes by cab from Agami. She brings pieces of our former lives from our flat—drawings from our bedroom walls, photographs we have forgotten. Once, she brought a stack of letters in my mother's handwriting. She gave them to me to read while my mother was at work. There were four letters addressed to Pa, all marked returned to sender. The first, when she got engaged, was an invitation to the wedding. She describes her fiancé as someone he would like: a Muslim man with strong values. The second was sent when Mohamed was born. *You have a grandson now*, she wrote. The third when I was born, *a granddaughter*, and the fourth, *Meet Aisha*.

You can hate me. I don't blame you. But please meet your grandchildren. They are your grandchildren. Nothing to do with me.

My grandfather began contacting my mother after the death of his wife—the woman he married after Nana left him. He sent chain mail, mostly, or news clippings about the Egyptian president. He mentioned coming to Melbourne, to visit the mosque he designed when he lived here. He said he had a Corvette, or maybe it was a Lamborghini—something worth a mint. He wanted to know if he could send it to Australia for safekeeping. My mother told him that she didn't have room for the car, but he was welcome to visit. He just had to let her know when, so she could make sure Nana was out of the house.

"I want him to come and see you kids," said my mother to me. I was not sure I shared her enthusiasm. She told me he would come on three conditions. "The first," she announced, "is that I prove I'm a good Muslim."

She said this as if it were reasonable. As though she might record herself praying five times a day. Skype him *at fajr, zuhr, asr, maghrib* and *isha*. Or do a medical test. Surely the Good Muslim gene was detectable in her blood. Hereditary, maybe.

"The second," she continued, "is that my children be good Muslims."

I rolled my eyes.

"And the third," she said, "is, because I am a single woman now"—she had told him about the divorce—"I need to give him control of my finances."

"Oh, fuck off!" shouted Nana from the living room. She could hear very well when she wanted to.

When Pa dies, he is alone, his wife gone, none of his family in his life. His death is from cancer, in his colon, his liver and his lungs. He had told my mother a couple months earlier, over text, that he was going to have an operation to cut it out.

"I asked him if he wanted me to go and see him, but he said no, he was fine, and that it wasn't a big deal," she says.

Nana is in Egypt when he dies, and various people at the hospital funnel information to her. The day before he dies, he is feeling fine and looks like he is improving, according to the people. My mother says this is common when someone is about to go—they perk up and look better than they have in weeks. It's a cruel trick of nature. Nana never went to see him, because she hates his guts, but she cries for two days when she hears he is dead. I don't see my mother cry once. When I ask her if she is okay, she says she lost her father thirty years ago, when he stopped speaking to her. She never uses the word "disowned".

When she finds out that he was refusing chemotherapy because he thought it would give him hepatitis, she is furious. "If I had known how bad it was, I would have ignored him, and I would have gone to Alexandria."

Nana visits his flat in Alexandria. She tells us it is full of empty water bottles, yoghurt containers and reams of unused paper. Nana thinks about donating the paper to the university. *They probably don't need it*, texts my mother, *they use computers now*. There are twenty jars of minced garlic in the fridge. That's what he thought was keeping him alive.

His late wife's sister is at the flat, too. She knows of a safe hidden in one of the walls. It holds her sister's jewellery, which my grandfather inherited. She believes it rightfully hers. She is looking for it, knocking on the walls to check if they are hollow. In the meantime, Nana wades through the rubbish, which is overwhelming. The only clean space in the house is his desk. On it, Nana says she is surprised to find a picture of my teenaged mother when she was in boarding school, with big teeth and frizzy hair. She takes a photo of the desk and texts it to us.

Later, she hears the sister of the late wife had gone back to the house alone. The next picture Nana sends is of a massive hole in a wall, and an empty safe.

❧ ❧ ❧ RULE NO. 3 ❧ ❧ ❧

ALWAYS TELL THE TRUTH

I WAS EIGHT WHEN NANA taught me to lie. Not big lies, just white lies. Little ones, which no one would ever discover. It began when she gave me a diary and told me to write in it every day.

Today I went shopping with Mama.

Today Mohamed bugged me.

Today Aisha did a big poo in her Pampers. It was too big for the Pampers and went up her back.

One particularly hot day, when the grass was sharp and the sun would not let up, Nana told the three of us kids to get outside. We went into the front yard and began squirting each other with the hose. Aisha was running around in my school hat. Mohamed was shooting water into the back of his throat, making himself gag, on repeat.

Newly bloomed jasmine hung in the air. A butterfly hovered around us and flew right up to me—right near my face. Close enough for me to see the veins of blue-grey in its delicate little wings. I told Nana about it.

"Write that in your diary," she said.

And so I did. At the end of the day I opened up my diary to a crisp new page and wrote: *Today I was playing outside and a butterfly flew right near my face.* I showed Nana.

"That's not what happened," she said.

I looked up at my grandmother. "Yes, it is," I said.

"That's a bit boring, isn't it? Write something better."

"Like what?"

"Wouldn't it be interesting," she said, "if the butterfly flew up to you and kissed your cheek?"

"Butterflies don't kiss."

"Of course they do. Go on. Write that."

And so I did.

Today a butterfly flew right near my face and then kissed my cheek.

"See?" she said. "Now when you're older and you pick up your diary and read that page, you'll think, 'Wow, what an interesting day I had. What a full life I've lived.'"

❧ ❧ ❧

AFTER MY FIRST FEW WEEKS at Morningside Primary, I began to grow. First, a tummy. Mama had warned me about this. We were all destined to be fat—it was in our genes. Then I grew arm hair. Also in our genes. And, finally, something Mama hadn't warned me about: I developed a crush on a white boy.

It was easy enough to believe that it was possible for him to like me back. That despite how uncomfortable I was becoming in my own body, it would be temporary. That there would be a time when I would shed the fat and the hair.

How I hoped to Allah there was a beautiful butterfly in there somewhere.

His name was Isaac. He was outgoing, more so than the other boys in our class, which is why we got to know each other. He was the only one who talked to me.

He didn't have any friends. I didn't know why, exactly. He didn't have the same interests as the other boys—they spent their lunchtimes playing basketball, while Isaac preferred skipping rope or colouring in. It was a shame, I thought, because he was one of the tallest boys in our grade, so would probably be great at basketball. He found it hard to get along with the girls in class too. Perhaps because he was too loud. But I liked him, because he talked to me.

We became friends quickly, Isaac and me. He always chose me when we had group activities in class. Mr. R didn't seem to mind at all that Isaac and I were a boy and a girl sitting together. Becoming friends.

At 11 am each day the bell would ring, and kids would stream from their classrooms and into the sun for a break. One day I had money and so did Isaac. We made our way across the asphalt, which was wet and hot from summer rain. Droplets of water spotted my culottes, which were already too small for me. Isaac peered over my shoulder in the cafeteria line. I shrugged my shirt higher so my collar would cover the soft hairs that were growing on the back of my neck. He asked me what I was buying as he rubbed his fifty-cent coins together between his fingers. He said he was getting a bacon and cheese bun, and I should get one too because they were the best thing here. Isaac knew what was good and what wasn't. He had been at the school a year longer than me, which equated to a lot more cafeteria days.

It would have been too much effort to explain why I couldn't get a bacon and cheese bun.

Bacon is pig. Pig is haram, I would say.

What is haram? he would say.

Things Muslims can't eat, I would say.

What is a Muslim? he would say.

I am a Muslim.

I wasn't ready for that conversation.

So I told Isaac *maybe*. I placed my order, and the cafeteria lady turned and filled a bag of hot wedges with a gloved hand.

I waited for Isaac as he fumbled for more change in his pockets. His shorts rose midway up his thigh. The cafeteria lady tapped the counter impatiently. He traded the coins for a meat-speckled bun.

He only noticed that I hadn't got a scroll as he bit into his. I lied and said I couldn't afford one. So he reached into his pocket, gave me his change and said I should buy one tomorrow.

That was all it took.

That afternoon, I went home and drew Isaac in my diary. I drew his dark widow's peak, his long legs extending out of short shorts, and his lips, in an exaggerated pout. I dotted freckles all around his cheeks. On the other side of the page I drew myself. Same pouted lips, stretching out to touch his. *Me and Isaac*, I wrote, and circled our bodies in a love heart. I tucked my diary beneath my mattress.

The next day, Isaac was behind me in the cafeteria line again. He asked if I was going to get a scroll. The cafeteria lady waited for my answer as I deliberated in a quiet panic.

I looked at Isaac, peering at me in hope. *Yes*, I said, resolutely, and she handed me the greasy bun.

We sat down in the shadow of the sport shed that allowed just enough shade for two.

"I have an idea for a game," I said. "It's called Who Do You Like? You have to whisper who you like to the other person."

Isaac looked suspicious. "Err. That's not really a game," he said.

"Yes it is."

"I'll only play if the rule is you're not allowed to tell."

"Okay."

"Anyone."

"Okay."

"You go first."

"No. You go first. That's the other rule."

"Okay." He leant over and whispered in my ear, "*Lilly.*"

I couldn't tell if he meant it. I had seen his interactions with Lilly. She was nasty to him—not letting him touch her colouring pencils in class, making fun of the way he jumped rope. Then he leant back and bit into the scroll. "Okay," he said, mouth still full, "your turn."

"*No one,*" I lied.

❧ ❧ ❧

MAMA WAS AT UNIVERSITY AGAIN. She was doing her master's so that she could practise as a doctor in Australia, or that's what she told me. The technicalities confused me—it seemed as though she had to start from scratch, even though she was already a doctor in Egypt.

That afternoon, she had an exam and couldn't pick us up from school. From my classroom, I could hear Baba's van idling outside the gate. It was off-white, with brown doors and seats that smelled like the old men who had owned it before.

The scroll was stowed in my bag; I'd pretended I was full. When Isaac left, I threw it in the bin.

Baba was wearing his hi-vis vest and reflective sunglasses, so all I could see in his eyes was a warped reflection of my face. I jumped in the front passenger side. The remnants of bacon stench hovered in my bag, so I kicked it under the seat. I was starving. I checked Baba's lunch esky while we waited for Mohamed. It was empty.

"I need to talk to you when we get home," he said.

I pretended to be still searching the esky. "About what?" I said. I could tell from his tone that it was not good news.

Mohamed opened the passenger door. "Hey!" he shouted at me. "I bagsed the front seat this morning!" He slammed it in my face.

"About what?" I said to Baba.

"When we get home," he said.

Baba didn't often come into my room, which I shared with Mohamed. When he did, it was to ask where I had put the television remote. But that day he came in and stood at the end of my bed. The mattress sank deeply when he sat. He looked uncomfortable. His sleeves were rolled up, his mangrove arm hair exposed. "I need to talk to you about something important." He had taken off his sunglasses, and he was looking me right in the eye. "Are you making friends at school?"

"Yes," I said.

"Girl friends? Do you play with girls?"

"I do, sometimes. But they don't always want to play with me. Lilly hates me."

"Try to be more friends with them." He shuffled awkwardly on the bed. The edge of my diary was still hidden under the mattress.

I was quiet.

"Because it's not good," he continued, "to play with boys."

I felt as though someone had stuffed a hot rag in my mouth. I always had a feeling my father was omniscient. It was as if he had hired a satellite in the sky to track me. Making sure I didn't break the rules.

"And absolutely no kissing boys."

My parents had never discussed it with me before, but I knew the rule as if it had been branded on my skin at birth. No boys. At all. Kissing is haram, unless it is your husband.

"I didn't," I said. I couldn't swallow. "It was a lie I wrote just for fun in my diary. So I could look back and remember an interesting thing."

"No more friends with boys. No more talking to boys. Okay? That's it." And he left my room.

He had found my diary. I didn't know how. I doubted Nana had told him about it. She had her own collection of white lies tucked under the mattress. Her own stories. She understood, I thought. He must have found it when he was looking for the remote. Or smelled the bacon in the car. Or seen Isaac say goodbye when he arrived to pick me up. But it didn't really matter how he knew. Just that he did.

I waited until Mohamed was playing Xbox in our room, and Nana was feeding Aisha in the kitchen, to find Baba in the living room.

"What if I marry him," I said. He was watching the Egyptian news channel, and I hoped he wouldn't turn around. He didn't.

"What?" said Baba, over his shoulder. "Marry who?"

"The boy at school. If I marry him, then I can kiss him?"

"No, you cannot marry him," he said with a laugh.

"Why not?"

"You are too young."

"Not now. Later. When I'm old enough."

"No, *habib*, you will marry someone like you. You are a Muslim girl, and Muslim girls marry Muslim boys."

"But I don't know any Muslim boys. I only know Mohamed."

The sound of *Halo* penetrated the walls.

He laughed again. "You cannot marry your brother, either."

"Who can I marry?"

"A good Muslim boy. Someone you meet at the mosque." He turned the TV up.

I returned to my room and pulled my diary out from under the mattress. I was embarrassed, now, that I had ever thought this was a good hiding spot. That I had thought there was such a thing as a good hiding spot in this family. I flicked through the pages, too afraid to read what I had written. How many times had he looked in it? How many lies had he seen? And how many had he mistaken as true? They were all stories, nothing but stories.

I opened to the page where I had drawn me and Isaac. It was him, on that page, with his widow's peak and his long legs and his freckled face. But it wasn't me. The girl I had drawn kissing him was thin and had smooth, straight hair that shimmied down her back like a bridal veil. She had skinny arms that reached out to Isaac, a delicate hand that touched the tips of his fingers. His greasy cheese-and-bacon fingers.

I shut the diary. The thought of ever opening it again made me retch.

MAMA

THE QUESTION "WHERE ARE YOU FROM?" is a curious one. Some people get offended by it. Some people need to know the answer to understand a family. I would like to ask my mother this question. *Where are you from, Mama?*

My mother has no accent. This became clear to me not long after we arrived in Australia, when I'd hear her speak with other mothers. Their voices were distinct—their consonants nasal, their vowels long. But my mother, her voice was neutral, her words flat and sharp. Her voice is from nowhere. It has no story.

"What's for tea?" says the checkout lady at Woolworths. I'm loading the groceries onto the belt with my mother. I like shopping with her. It's nice to spend time together, even if all we talk about is the price of grapes or which brand of frozen chips is better.

"Sorry?" says my mother. She couldn't hear the woman over the store intercom announcing that Tim Tams were on special.

"What's for tea? You've got some interesting ingredients here." Australians speak in their own way. They have their own words. *Tea* means dinner. *Ta* means thanks. *Tim Tam* means chocolate biscuit.

If my mother did have an accent, it would be an amalgam of the places she's lived. She was born in Egypt. When she was three, she moved to Melbourne. When she was ten, she returned to Egypt and went to a boarding school. When she was sixteen, she lived in America on exchange. When she was thirty-five, she moved to Brisbane. But none of this past is detectable in her voice.

"Oh," says my mother. She hates these questions, because if she answers, it inevitably leads to more questions. We're having *messa'aa*, but this would mean nothing to the check-out lady. So she says, "Eggplant … bake."

Bake. Another Australian word. Everything that goes into the oven is a bake. This borrowed word sounds strange in my mother's mouth.

We pack the bags into the trolley. The lady hands Mama the receipt. "Thanks," says my mother. She does not say "ta."

I've gotten into the habit of double-booking myself. Not intentionally—I just don't want to disappoint either of my parents, and my mother has a habit of thinking I will be at the house every night for dinner, even though she knows logically that sometimes I will have to visit Baba. It's my fault, because sometimes I don't have the heart to tell her I won't be eating her food. She doesn't talk to Baba. She hasn't since the divorce, but sometimes she talks about him. This is another word that stands out in her otherwise uninflected words. She says it like this: *faaatha*. As if she's putting on a mock Australian accent. But that's just how she says it. *Faaatha.* The word is unnatural in her mouth, just like *bake*.

She tells me that my father isn't a bad man, they're just
different. This sounds like something someone in a movie
would say: *We just didn't fit together.* I want to know why they
didn't know that from the beginning. My father carries the
place he is from in his voice. You can see it in his home. The
woven carpet. The open Qur'an. The smell of kofta spices
in his kitchen on Sunday afternoon. He doesn't hide it. He
would say *messa'aa* and expect people to figure it out. But my
mother is different.

At home, she ties her hair up in a high bun. She does this
when she cooks so her neck doesn't get too hot. I understand,
because we have similar hair. Nana likes to peer over Mama
as she cooks. She often surveys in this way. Mama looks
nothing like Nana, but everything like her father. I am told
this over and over. This man I never met held the only evidence of where my mother is from, beyond city or country.
He was the only lead to her story.

I have to go, because Baba is waiting for me.

"Enjoy your time with your faaatha," she says. It doesn't
sound genuine.

BABA

I WATCH MY FATHER EAT his dry chicken breast in Kofta Burger. We've developed a habit of coming here after his treatment because it is nearby and halal, and he has started to eat only halal meat again. He ordered the chicken despite the doctor telling him he needs to double his red-meat intake to replace his blood cell loss. My father says there's no point in eating the meat at Kofta Burger because there's no blood in it anyway.

Two kids are jumping on the seat in the booth behind us. My father's mouth slides down. In Arabic, he says he wants to punch them. Their mother pretends not to sense his anger. I tell him to calm down.

We came in my car because he wasn't sure if he could drive, but now he insists on driving. He hardly readjusts the driver's seat, his puffer vest pushing up to his chin as he squeezes into the space I usually take. A prayer is muttered, a key is turned, and he backs out without looking.

Soon he is doing forty under the limit, in the middle of the road. A car edges past and honks.

"Hey, you facking idiot," my father yells out the window. The driver flips him off. My father doesn't see it, because if he did, I would have known. I tell him again to calm down.

My father never swore when my parents were together. It was only afterwards he started incorporating these new words into his vocabulary. It feels like an acknowledgement that I am now adult enough to handle it. To understand.

We stop at the petrol station because I'm almost on empty. He asks me why I'm always running the tank down, and I ignore him. I get out and fill up with '95.

"Eh da? Why '95? Ninety-eight is always better."

"Ninety-five is cheaper," I say.

He shakes his head. "Always about money, just like your facking mother."

The driveway of his temporary accommodation is long, shared with a couple of other townhouses. The place is rented for the week, while he is here getting his chemo. I get out of the car and say goodbye.

He asks me if I want to come in for some tea, so I do.

He says it's not him, it's the chemicals. They muddy his blood and muddle his mind.

I boil the kettle, make us tea, and we sit together for a time.

NO MOVING OUT WITHOUT A HUSBAND

MAMA GOT ASTHMA BECAUSE OF Nana. It wasn't hereditary; Nana didn't give her asthma in that sense. But she definitely caused it. When Mama was sixteen, she was staying at her mother's house in Agami. She was there for the summer holidays, having just returned from a year-long exchange in America. Agami is a beachy place. With a beach comes heat, and with heat comes bugs. That summer, the bugs in the house had gotten so bad that Nana couldn't take it. She closed all the windows and all the doors, and emptied a whole can of bug spray. And that's when Mama had her first asthma attack. The spray filled her lungs and she was on the ground, struggling to breathe. Nana left Mama gagging and ran outside in a panic. She ran to the house of a doctor she knew, who lived on the other side of the town.

I often think about how Mama would have felt, alone in that house, while her mother ran through the streets to get help. There was no one to sit with her, to tell her that she wouldn't suffocate. She just had to wait and see if her mother would come through. I wonder if she thought that was the end.

Eventually, Nana came back with the doctor, who had Ventolin, and Mama recovered in no time. It's a funny story, and the punchline is chronic lung disease.

❦ ❦ ❦

IN 2003, NANA GOT HER own flat. At first I thought it was because she wanted her own space, and in a way that was true. She liked having her own kitchen, with her own small fridge. Her own living room, with her own two-seater couch. And her own balcony, from which we could see the fireworks on New Year's Eve, even if they were so far away they looked like embers on a neighbour's cigarette. She had lived with us since we moved to Australia, more than a year before, but it was time for her to be on her own.

This sudden grab for independence was an inconvenience to Mama, who worked unsociable hours interning at the hospital and needed Nana's help. So every morning, my siblings and I would wake up, teeth not brushed, breakfast not had, eyes not open, and tumble into the car. At Nana's place, we would tumble out again, and be washed, brushed and fed. Mohamed and I were sent off to school, which was a short walk from the block of flats. Aisha was too young for school, so she and Nana would spend the whole day together. Oxford Street in Bulimba was their main hangout, where they both had babyccinos at Riverbend bookshop, followed by a walk to the park or the library. They'd be back at the apartment by the time Mohamed and I returned.

When we'd get home each evening, back to Mama and Baba, Aisha would tell our parents about her day with Nana. "When we were walking to the café," the three-year-old said once, "the pam cacked" (the pram cracked) "and the man" (in the shop they had broken down in front of) "said, 'I can fix it'—but he didn't have a hammer!" *Classic man, making promises he can't keep,* Nana would add. "So, he gave us a new one!"

Baba found this story amusing. So amusing, he repeated it often. "When we were walking to the café, the pam cacked," he'd say, in mimic. The story of the cacked pam and the man with promises who saved the day became family folklore.

We spent more time at Nana's flat than we did at our house. On the shared driveway, we drew chalk landscapes, we burst water balloons, we threw Halloween parties all year round. According to Nana, none of the other residents in the block cared as long as we were having fun.

On summer holidays, we could bring our friends to Nana's house. Mohamed often played Xbox with boys on the tiny TV that was mounted to the wall, the air conditioning blasting. Australia had strange weather—even when it was blistering hot, rain clouds sometimes hovered, threatening to let loose.

Because Nana didn't drive, she walked, caught the bus or got lifts everywhere. It was for the best that she didn't drive, because I couldn't imagine Nana following road rules. I couldn't, for example, see her stopping at a red light, or driving on the left side of the road, or respecting the boundaries of a footpath just because it was what you were supposed to do. She hated being told what to do. 'I spent my whole marriage with your grandfather being told what to do. I will do whatever the bloody hell I please.'

Nana had had many men in her life. She was married more than once. I'm not sure exactly how many times, but they all ended. Her first marriage, to my grandfather, was the one I have heard most about. They met at university. They hadn't known each other for very long before they got engaged. Pictures of their wedding show Nana in a gown adorned with lace, which had been handmade and imported from England. She still keeps these pictures in an album. Whenever we pull them out, she's sure to remind us all of how ugly her ex-husband was. "My wedding dress, though," says Nana, "was the most beautiful thing I ever saw."

Nana was born in Cambridge to an English mother and an Egyptian father. They had met at university too. Her mother converted to Islam, and they moved to Alexandria when Nana was two. There are pictures of her parents in the album as well. Her mother, white as a lily. Her father, the epitome of tall, dark and handsome. Her father died not long after Mama was born. She recounted their last meeting: *"Darling. Sweetheart. Don't you have any clothes?"* Nana mimicked the gesture he made with his glass towards her outfit. Whisky was in his glass, she reminded us. "Of course there was none of this backward 'no alcohol' business back then," said Nana. "He asked if I had the money to buy something new. *I don't need new clothes. I'm comfortable enough,* I said. But I wasn't. Not at all. Never let your husband touch your money. Never let a man touch your money. You hear me? Never."

One overcast day, Nana packed Aisha into the pram. Mohamed had friends over to play Xbox. On their way out, they crossed paths with one of Mohamed's friends and his father, dropping him off.

"It looks like it might rain," said the father.

"I know. But I have to get out. Can't stay in all day! Or I'll suffocate," said Nana with a coquettish laugh.

Aisha let out a cough that sounded like she was getting a cold. The man looked concerned. "Okay," he said, "well, how 'bout this. On my way to collect the boy this afternoon, I'll pick you girls up from the park. That way, you get home before it starts."

"Oh, would you? That would be lovely."

The air was so humid it was hard to breathe. The walk from the apartment to the café usually took half an hour, but Aisha was so overheated and restless they had to detour into shops every few minutes, for the air conditioning. The shopkeepers would look at Nana as she stood there, buying nothing, sticky hair drying, not even pretending to browse.

Once they reached the café, they ordered a babyccino for Aisha and, this time, a large mug of English breakfast for Nana. Two tea bags. No sugar. Milk on the side. She liked her tea brewed strong, extra strong. Nothing was worse than too-white tea.

Afterwards, they walked to the park. They kept their pace up because the man would be there to pick them up soon. They wouldn't have much time to spend at the park, but at least they would have a ride home.

The clouds were dark when they arrived at the playground, and it was starting to spit. Nana sat on a platform, part of the play equipment, to shelter from the rain. Aisha sat in her pram, coughing the hot air from her lungs. The mesh canopy above started dripping.

Nana and Aisha were abandoned in the park during the torrential rainstorm. They were stuck standing under the canopy, waiting for the man who had made a promise. Nana could have walked to the shop nearby and called my father. He would have been home. It was the weekend, and he had a car. But she didn't. She waited for the man.

He eventually showed up, two hours late.

"How are we, girls? Bit wet out. Told you!" said the man as he folded and packed the pram into the boot of his car, not acknowledging his tardiness.

"There's something about men," Nana has said to me, "that makes me hate them. They are bossy. They are controlling. They are rude. They say one thing and they do another. They make rules for you and then follow none of them. They are hypocrites. They take, they take, they take, and give you nothing but a headache. Men are pigs, all of them. Don't get married, if you can help it."

When Aisha came home spluttering, it was easy to make it seem like Nana's fault. After all, she was the one who had insisted on going out. She was the one who went to the park instead of staying at the café. She was the one who relied on the man to pick them up on time instead of having her own car. It was all Nana's fault.

❧ ❧ ❧

THE TRUTH IS THAT NANA didn't move out of our house because she wanted to. She moved out because Baba told her to.

"We were in the car," said Nana, "going to the supermarket, and your father was going on and on and on about Islam. How Islam is the greatest religion, and everyone should be a Muslim. And I said, well, just hold on a minute. Not *everyone* has to be a Muslim. I'm a Muslim too, you know, and I don't think *everyone* should be a Muslim. People can jolly well be whatever they like. And he didn't like that. We had a big row."

Despite only living the first two years of her life in England, Nana had a posh accent. As always, it was her word against his.

Baba blamed Nana for a lot of problems that were occurring in our household, and particularly for inspiring her daughter with ideas of the single life. She had somehow lodged the idea that marriage was suffocating. That not only could Mama live without him, but it was impossible to live with him. Nana convinced Mama that having a husband was killing her, and she had to get out.

"Imagine," Baba says to me, "living with your mother-in-law your whole life as a married man. Not across the neighbourhood. Not across the street. Not as a next-door neighbour. Living *with* her. It's not good for the marriage. It's a nightmare."

And now here is the real punchline. That man, that father of Mohamed's friend who left Nana and Aisha out in the rain for two hours, went on to become a very senior Australian politician. *Walahi*, swear to god. It's a funny story. That's how we tell it.

BABA

I'M UNPACKING HIS BAGS. He has signed a lease on an apartment so he can have somewhere more permanent to stay when he comes for his treatments. A familiar place. With him is a shopping bag full of little clumps of spinach, left over from different meals on different days and packaged into individual bags. There is a ziplock of defrosting cooked meat.

"You have ten boxes of figs," I say. "Why?"

"Ten? I do not have ten."

"Look." I pile them up.

"I bought seven because they were only one-ninety-five each."

"Okay. But, I mean, there are a lot."

"But not ten." He takes a box and rinses the figs. "Come have some. They are lovely."

I sit with my father on the couch.

"The dark ones are better," he says, handing me the one he has just bitten and beckoning for the lighter one I am holding.

The house is plain and relatively empty. There is a box of fragiles on the floor. People say a strong man, a healthy man, can rip a telephone book in half. My father has carefully wrapped each of his cups and his plates in a single leaf from the Yellow Pages.

I take the cups out and place them in the cupboard. I push the plain ones to the back and keep the brightly coloured ones at the front.

"I want to make this look nice," I say, adjusting a floral mug so the flowers show.

"Thank you, habib."

I turn the mugs so they are in couples, with the curved handles touching. I stack the plates, which are all white, in two piles. Once I'm done, I fill the box with the crumpled Yellow Pages.

My father is thin these days. The thinnest I've ever seen him. He looks weak when he walks, as though his bones could splinter at the slightest touch.

"Do you want some tea?" he asks, as I start to head out to the recycling bin. "Where is my favourite mug?"

"Which one?"

"It has *bismillah*."

I know the one—it is a white mug with brown scripture on it. I put the box down and reach in the cupboard, to the third row, and grab it.

"No!" he says when I pass it to him. The handle has broken.

"I didn't even see that."

"Oh no. My favourite."

"Sorry."

"*Khad el sharr*," he says. This is something we say when things break. It takes the evil away. He throws the broken mug in the box, and it shatters in two.

DON'T PLAY ALLAH

THE MATRIARCH OF THE FAMILY had red lips and big tits. No, pink lips. Pink lips and a boob tube. A miniskirt and high heels that she could wear all day. She had long brown hair, half up, half down. She was turned on by vampires, turned off by cologne. Her aspiration was Family: she wanted a husband and kids. She was a Gemini. I twirled her around in the dressing room to make sure I had everything right. I blinked, the first blink in some time. I was ready to build my patriarch in *The Sims* when Baba called for me from the living room. His friend from the mosque had arrived. I didn't answer, but with the second loud boom I peeled myself from the chair, my mind still on my Sim family.

His friend had a thin black combover, stubble, a pot-belly and a poorly ironed grey-and-blue check shirt. He was laughing at something my father had said, one hand on Baba's shoulder like they'd known each other a lifetime. But they had only met when they stood next to each other at Friday prayer two weeks ago. His aspiration, I imagined, was Popularity. Wanting to have as many friends as possible. In other people's houses as often as he could be. A real schmooze.

The schmooze came with a daughter, which is why my father had called me. She was wearing a floral dress that skimmed the ground. On her head was a delicate white hijab. I would've picked floral, to match the dress, if she were my Sim. She was taller than me, and closer to my brother's age than mine. Her thick eyebrows had no curve to them, sitting straight across her forehead. She didn't make eye contact. I knew immediately that she didn't like me. We both knew that she was a better Muslim than I was.

"Hello, hello," her father said. He was talking to me on her behalf, a dummy with his ventriloquist.

"Soos, this is Fatima," said Baba. "Take Fatima and go and play."

I stared at him. My eyes said, *please don't make me*, but he ignored them. We were always taught to be nice to our guests, and to do what we could to make them happy. That included things that would make us unhappy.

"Go and show her your room," he said.

"She doesn't want to see my room."

"Go show her your toys. Your new book. That one you like so much."

Fatima smelled like strawberry liquorice perfume—the knock-off kind, that would have the word *Beyonce* in cursive written on the bottle and would end up in a lawsuit.

As soon as we left the living room, it started.

"I'm bored," she said, picking at the edge of her scarf. "What's this book your dad was talking about? Sounds boring."

I pulled the book out from under my bed. It was blue, with a smiling sunflower on the front. It was a friendship book that came loaded with questions. Each page was a profile waiting to be created. I had only filled out the first page, about Mama. What's her favourite colour? Green or blue. What's her best feature? Her hair. What's my favourite thing about her? She washes my bum for me sometimes with the *shatafa,* the hose cut-off we used as a substitute for a bidet. Even for a nine-year-old, it was hard to get into all the nooks and crannies. I flicked past the first page quickly and opened to the second.

"You fill out the questions," I told her.

"Aren't you supposed to fill them out for me?" she said.

"I don't know the answers."

"You're meant to ask me. Duh."

I pushed the pen towards her. "It's quicker if you fill it out."

The Sims jingle was still playing faintly from the computer down the hall. I watched her write slowly, thinking on each question. As if she knew nothing about herself. As if she was making it up on the spot. I started designing my patriarch in my head. Tanned skin, muscles. Turn on, make-up. Turn off, perfume. Strawberry liquorice.

Underneath the question *What do they want to be when they grow up?* Fatima wrote, *A millionaire.*

My patriarch's aspiration would be Fortune.

"Do you want to play on the computer?" I asked her.

"Play what?"

"I was playing *The Sims* before you came. We could play that."

"No." She shut the book.

"It's one-player, but we can share."

"That game is bad."

I was surprised. "Who said?"

"Um. It's haram. Duh."

"Says who?"

"It's playing God. You can't make people and control what they do. That's Allah's job."

"That's not true."

"Yes it is."

"It's just a game."

"You can't say it's right when it's wrong just because it's a game. Ask my dad."

❦ ❦ ❦

MY PARENTS HAD A LONG-RUNNING rule that I was not allowed sleepovers at other people's houses. They were afraid something would happen to me. Essentially, they were afraid I would get raped. They never said this outright, and it would be uncomfortable for them to explain, so they just banned sleepovers.

Fatima became the only person I was allowed to break that rule with. She asked my father and he said yes, just like that. "Of course, habibi."

"But," I said, "I thought we weren't allowed."

"Fatima is fine," said Baba. "She is a good girl."

I was fuming.

Late that night, she was in my bed, I was in Mohamed's bed, and Mohamed was in the living room, sleeping on the floor. But Fatima, she did not sleep. She also did not, for a moment, shut her mouth. She was talking about *Home and Away*.

Describing the characters as if they were real people, ones she knew. As soon as I'd start to drift off, she would raise her voice in excitement. I imagined taking her long brown ponytail and stuffing it in her mouth.

"I'm hungry," she said suddenly. It was late. Everyone else in the house was asleep.

"Can you wait until the morning?" I said.

"No. Get me something to eat? Yalla, good girl." She spoke like an aunty, like I had to do what she said. Just because she was older.

In our house, once Baba went to bed, that was it. There was no getting up in the middle of the night. There was no going to the kitchen in the dark. There was no pulling out the bowl of cherries that was meant to be for everyone. But there I was, in the glow of the fridge. I imagined Mohamed waking up and seeing a figure and screaming, my parents running in thinking I was a thief, the police bursting in with the commotion and shooting me dead. All because Fatima couldn't wait until morning.

When I got back to the bedroom, the light was on.

"Does your mum still wash your ass?" she said, my book in her hands. I didn't say anything. "Your mum sticks her hand up your ass? Ech."

She ate half the bowl of cherries and then, finally, fell asleep.

Full and satisfied. A stupid grin on her face.

I didn't want to see Fatima again, but I had to, because she woke up in my bed. Mama would have noticed that the bowl of cherries was missing from the fridge, but she said nothing. Instead, she made scrambled eggs for everyone.

"I want an omelette," said Fatima.

"*Hardir*," Mama said. Right away. Like a servant. And went back to the kitchen to crack another egg.

Her father showed up at midday. I hovered near him, hoping to offload his daughter quickly, but he sat at the dining table, meaning he would be there for some time.

"Why don't you play your picture game with Fatima?" said Baba.

"What picture game?" she said.

"Pictionary," I said. "But you need more people for teams."

"What's your brother doing?" Fatima asked. She already knew where he was. She walked down the hall and into our room. Mohamed was on the floor, playing his Xbox.

"Hey, Mohamed. Do you want to play Pictionary with us?"

"Not really," he said. But he sighed and paused his game, because he had to. I pulled the box off our shelf and took it out to the dining table. I needed to keep Fatima in her father's sight to make sure he remembered to take her home. "We need one more player," I said.

"Uncle, will you play?" said Fatima to Baba. He smiled and nodded, mid-sentence, in conversation with her father. He didn't fully understand what he was agreeing to, I could tell, but that did not stop him doing as he was told.

Fatima and I formed one team, Baba and Mohamed the other. Mohamed was picking his nails under the tablecloth as Fatima and I had our turn. The word was *carpenter*. I drew a stick figure with a saw, standing next to a table and a tree stump.

"Man?" she said.

"No."

"Cutting?"

"No."

"Tree?"

"No."

"Wood?"

"No."

The timer ran out.

"It was *carpenter*," I said.

She looked confused. "Then where is the carpet? You should have drawn a carpet."

"*Carpenter*. Why would I draw a carpet for a carpenter?"

Her father interjected. "No, habibi," he said to his daughter, "carpenter can also mean someone who works with wood."

I saw both Mohamed's and Baba's eyebrows jerk up at the word *also*. I imagine mine did too. She was wrong. Completely wrong. And he was too scared to tell her.

"Oh. Okay," she said. "So, you just drew a confusing thing then. Next time just draw a carpet. Duh."

"Let's move on," said Baba quickly.

"I don't want to play," said Mohamed, not because he cared about the injustice that had taken place, but because he was bored. He jumped off the seat and headed back to the bedroom.

"Do you want to try another card?" I said to Fatima.

"What's the point?" she said. "No one wants to play." And she followed Mohamed back to the room.

I packed up the cards. When I entered our room, Mohamed was mid eyeroll, handing her the controller to his Xbox. And that is when I had enough. "I don't care what you say!" I said. "I'm going to play Sims. I don't care what you and your dad say."

"Whatever," she said, her eyes not leaving the television screen. "You're the one who will have to answer to Allah on the Day of Judgement."

I stood in the doorway, frozen. She had me.

My brother and I watched Fatima kick her *Mortal Kombat* opponent in the head repeatedly. Eventually, she got bored and asked her dad if they could go home.

"We'll see you at the mosque soon, eh, Soos?" said her father as they were leaving. A familiar pang of guilt hit me. It was the same one I felt every Friday when Baba went and I made up an excuse like I was tired or I was sick or I had homework. Fatima looked at me as though she knew what I was thinking. She was a Good Muslim, and I wasn't.

There is a secret aspiration in *The Sims*. It's the Power aspiration. I found out about it when looking up cheats. You have to enter a special code to get it. Sims bestowed with this aspiration seek a mix of Popularity and Fortune, and to control the Sims around them. They gain pleasure from giving orders and telling people what to do, influencing others to the extent that their lives are controlled not by will but by command. This secret aspiration was never fully developed by the game-makers. It caused glitches—Sims with this aspiration would be perpetually unfulfilled because it was impossible to achieve real Power. There was only one Sim that possessed a fully realised Power aspiration: the Grim Reaper, the hooded figure that descended on the neighbourhood when it was time for a Sim to die. He was the only one with the ability to truly control lives. And no one could play the Grim Reaper. But I did try to make my Sim have sex with him once, unsuccessfully.

So, there I was playing God, trying to bump uglies with Satan, while good girls like Fatima were at the mosque. And that thought made me hate myself.

MAMA

I FIND MYSELF WANTING TO ask my mother why her father disowned her. The timing doesn't feel right—she's building a chicken coop in her garden, and I'm watching through the window. She labours on it every morning before work. Today she's putting in a miniature picket fence around the coop. There's a can of white paint nearby, ready. She will not be getting a rooster, because the chickens will be for eggs only.

Even if I did ask about her father, I doubt I would get a direct answer. Mama doesn't like talking about serious things. She's the type of person to get a hysterectomy and not tell anyone about it beforehand: she will say she's popping off to Woolworths and then get a body part removed. While Baba is very open about his health, Mama is a locked door, and that scares me.

Everything I know about my mother I have learned from Nana, because Nana has no problem talking. Once Mama has left for work, Nana wanders out to the chicken coop. Since it's empty, she's not going to visit any chickens—she's just going to inspect her daughter's work. The same way she inspects her cooking. I follow her, and because it's quiet, I ask.

"Let's start from the beginning," Nana says. When she speaks, she sways from side to side with the rhythm of her own voice, and touches her thumb to each finger on her right hand, like she's counting her memories, or keeping a beat. "When we were in Melbourne—you know we lived in Melbourne in the seventies?"

"Yeah."

"Well, I was so depressed there. I had had enough of your grandfather. I hated him, I really did. You know he didn't let me do anything? He controlled all my money. My wages went right into his bank account!"

"Yep, you've told me, Nana."

"He was all about money. Money, money, money, money."

"I thought he stopped talking to her way after you left him?" I said.

"Yes, yes, hold on. I'm getting there. Leaving this man wasn't easy. Like I said, he wouldn't let me go anywhere. Even when my father died in Egypt, he wouldn't let me go to be with my mother. Can you imagine? Evil little man."

The beat on her fingers was steadily getting faster.

"So, I had to make a plan. I wrote a letter to my sister in Egypt. I wrote to her and I said, 'Can you write a letter back to me, telling me there's some inheritance issues I need to come and sort out, and that I have to go to Egypt to sort them out, and if I don't sort them out I won't get any money?' And she did. She wrote a letter back to me saying exactly that. And of course, because it was about money, your grandfather couldn't resist. He let me go. I packed as much stuff into one suitcase as I could, I grabbed your mother and I left."

"But he wasn't angry at Mama for that, was he?" I said. "How could he be? She was a child."

"Let me finish! Anyway. When we got to Egypt, I immediately wrote your grandfather a letter. A very simple letter, only four words: *I want a divorce.* I thought that was it. I had done it—I had gotten away from this wretched man. When his reply came in the mail, I opened it up, and it was very simple too. One word: *No.*"

Why would a man so adamant about keeping hold of his wife cut his daughter off? But Nana's blood sugar has dropped a little; I can tell by the changed rhythm of the swaying. She turns to go inside. She doesn't finish the story. She doesn't give me an answer.

When Mama gets back from work in the evening, she brings in bags. She's been to the shop on the way home and bought punnets of marigolds and beetroot sprouts, to be planted along the white picket fence. Marigolds and beetroot are apparently chickens' favourites. She's also bought another bucket of paint, the right kind this time—outdoor, not indoor.

I am scared of the things my mother does not tell me. We all keep our secrets from each other, but I wish she would tell me her mistakes so I could learn from them. I am made from my mother, after all. If something breaks for her, it may well break for me. If something is wrong inside her, chances are it's inside me too. I can't escape what's hereditary. But it's only natural to want to avoid the damage I can.

BABA

BABA STARTS HAVING ANTICIPATORY NAUSEA before going to the hospital, which doesn't sound sensible to me. He knows he will be sick soon, so he becomes sick now. I scroll through my phone while I wait for him. A prayer mat is hanging from the back of a dining-room chair. My knees haven't touched one in a very long time. It's possible that I have forgotten how to do it.

There is no such thing as a Bad Muslim, really, because if you are not a Good Muslim, you are not a Muslim at all. For me there has been an expiration.

The sound of my father's retching fills the house. There is another carpet on the floor—just a regular rug, not for prayer. He told me it was made in Palestine and it must be true, because it is so beautifully asymmetrical. He got it from eBay. It curls up at one corner, and I always forget this, tripping over it every time. When my father sees me trip, he reminds me that if I visited more often, I might remember to watch my step.

"Do you want to hear a funny story?" he says as he emerges from the bathroom, wiping his mouth and buttoning a fresh shirt. I check how long it will take to get to the hospital in current traffic. "Do you remember when you were small baby and you fell off the toilet?"

I do remember, but I can't tell if the memory is really mine or just because he has told this story so often. "You were leaning forward so far, and you fell off and hit your head on a tap, and the tap broke off! And you were crying and crying." He laughs.

"Yes, I remember," I say. "I was crying because no one came to help me."

"No, you were crying because you hit your head on the tap."

"We'd better get going."

"Okay. Let me *sulli*." He lays the prayer mat in front of the dining chair and sits to pray. He closes his eyes and raises his hands to his head. Then he stops. He opens one eye and looks at me. I look back. He gestures for me to move out of the way. I forgot—I am sitting to his east, obstructing his prayer to Mecca.

I go to the bathroom to pass the time. There are three toothbrushes in a cup. Toothbrushes are meant to be thrown out after three months. That's what they say on the packaging, which is still sitting in the bin next to the sink. These have been here much longer than that. Surely the three-month rule only applies if they're in use, though. I wet my face.

Baba's house is clean. He keeps it nice. He vacuums, and he mops, and he washes, all for himself. My father was never a slob, but I see him scrub at surfaces more now that he is in this house, where there is no one to impress with his cleanliness.

We get to the hospital and take a number. There are people here I have seen before. Some have deteriorated faster than others. My father is still plump compared to a woman in a purple crocheted hat, who started wearing the hat not when she lost her hair but when she lost her body fat. My father's number is called.

"It seems as though none of the nurses wants to work with you," the doctor says, when we are seated in his office. He sounds almost delighted, as if scaring nurses away is an endearing quirk.

"Who said?" asks my father. He doesn't see it that way. He holds out his arms. There is some bruising. "They use me like a cushion for pins. How would you feel? If someone does this to you?"

The doctor's grin disappears. "They said you were being difficult."

"All of them?"

"Yes, all of them."

"What about the tattoo nurse?"

"Rita," I say.

"Yes," says my father, "lovely Rita who found my vein. You don't believe me? Go and find her and ask her. She will tell you the other nurses were so bad. So bad."

The doctor grimaces.

"Rita will tell you the truth. Just like she said—all it takes is a little warmth and a little time. But no one here has this for me."

"Okay," says the doctor. "Give me a moment. I'll call for Rita." He leaves the room.

My father turns to me, a smile on his face. "Another funny story," he says. "When you were small baby, your mother dropped you on your head on the stairs at the train station!

That's why she doesn't wear skirts anymore, because she tripped on her skirt and dropped you down the stairs." He laughs. "Does she still not wear skirts?"

"Yeah."

He laughs, and I laugh too.

✿ ✿ ✿ **RULE NO. 6** ✿ ✿ ✿

NEVER LOCK YOUR DOOR

THERE IS NOTHING WORSE THAN being stuck. By 2004, we were starting to outgrow the house at Morningside. Mama and Baba had saved enough for the bank to finally let them take out a loan.

The loan was the easy part. Mama liked that about Australia. "In Egypt," she said, "you'd be in your grave by the time they looked at your application. Then they will take their lunch break."

Finding a place to live was not quick. Mama's idea of nice was Baba's idea of hideous. Baba's full-of-potential was Mama's full-of-shit. My parents spent the winter looking, warmed by hot tempers and scorching arguments.

Meanwhile, just as my siblings and I were trapped in a hothouse of our parents' discontent, I became trapped in a literal sense. The Morningside Flyers swim team moved training to the weekends, to the indoor pool complex a couple of blocks away from the school.

It was a particularly stuffy day in the complex. The steam from the pool made the windows fog and slathered condensation on skin and walls alike. Several squads of different age levels were training at the same time, so it was hard to tell which whistle belonged to which instructor, which squeal to which child. It was loud, what with kids kicking in the water, adults shouting at kids, and the ubiquitous buzz of the thermoelectric generator.

There was no shared changing room, which was a relief— only individual bathroom cubicles with doors that slid shut and left no crack. I shuffled into a cubicle with my bag of clothes and pulled the door shut behind me. A satisfying *click* came from the lock, as the hook slid into its strike. I pulled my wet costume off, feeling like a sausage bursting from its intestinal casing in a hot pan. I squeezed into the bralette Mama had recently bought me. I hadn't felt comfortable wearing it until the day I felt uncomfortable without it. Three sprigs of hair had appeared on my chest, now flattened and wet. I didn't want to imagine what someone like Lilly might say about chest hair on a girl. Nipples were at least somewhat expected. I put a dry t-shirt on, hoping no one had noticed them in the pool, and some shorts.

I was dressed and covered. No one could see my body anymore. Mama would be waiting for me outside by now.

I pinched the lock, trying to wiggle it open, but the humidity made it too slippery to manoeuvre. I shook the door, but it wouldn't budge, swollen shut in the heat.

The bathroom of the indoor swimming pool was a coffin. No one could hear me scream. When I called, my voice was sucked up by the high ceiling and out through the tiny window that I had no chance of reaching. I could hear the kids outside, splashing in the water. I imagined their wrinkled fingertips and chlorine-soaked faces, their hairless legs and flat bellies moving them through the water like slimy eels. I imagined pulling the plug on the pool and their bodies being sucked down in a whirl without being caught, without a snag. I tugged on the door until my arms were tired, the tips of my fingers sore from trying to grip the wood. I pulled down my shorts, because the toilet was the only place to sit and the seat was cool. I began to cry.

❧ ❧ ❧

I AM NOT THE ONLY one with a memory of being stuck in a bathroom. Baba has one too. He got trapped in the Morningside house while having a shower. The moist air swelling the door could have done it, as it did in my case. Or it could have been a faulty lock. Or perhaps the door just got jammed, as doors do from time to time. Afterwards, there were many theories.

The door wouldn't budge. The landlord eventually had to send a locksmith. He undid the lock with a screwdriver, jiggled the door a bit, and Baba was free. He emerged with fury. He'd missed his appointment, he yelled. A very important work meeting. All because of a stupid lock. Locked! In his own house. The locksmith gave him a sympathetic laugh, but there was nothing funny to Baba about being an angry Arab man in a towel. When the locksmith left, Baba went back into the bathroom to have another shower—the stress had made him perspire too much.

Mama was the only one home when Baba got stuck. She said she didn't hear him calling for at least the first hour. "It's hard to hear when you're in the kitchen." She was defensive.

"All the pots and pans. And your father takes long showers. How was I supposed to know he was stuck? He could have called out louder."

🐾 🐾 🐾

TWENTY MINUTES AFTER SWIMMING TRAINING had finished, Mama knocked on the cubicle. She asked if I was in there and I yelled out yes. She jiggled the door and it came free.

"Why didn't anyone look for me?" I cried.

"You could have opened the door."

"It was stuck."

"It wasn't stuck."

"It was. Why did you wait so long to come and find me?"

"That's enough, Soos." People were looking at us. "You're alive, aren't you?"

"I was trapped, and no one cares. No one ever cares."

"No, no one cares. Yalla, get in the car."

We sat in silence for a while, the heat cranked up. We slowed to a traffic light.

"What do you expect me to do?" Mama said. I didn't look at her. "Do you want me to stick to you twenty-four-seven in case you get stuck in the toilet? Am I meant to quit my job to follow you around all day because you might do something stupid? Am I meant to drop everything and come to your rescue every time you do something dumb? I am your mother, not your minder. I came eventually, didn't I? You are the one who got yourself stuck. Don't blame me for issues you cause yourself."

"You don't care that I was stuck," I said.

"It opened perfectly for me."

🐾 🐾 🐾

WHILE MAMA WAS IN THE kitchen, not hearing Baba, she noticed the flower of mould on the edge of the sink had started to reform, even though she'd sprayed it with bleach a week earlier. The house had a way of making problems reappear, no matter how hard she tried to solve them. One of the blinds had fallen off the rod. Baba had promised to fix it, but he hadn't. The plasterboard was cracking after a long spell of no rain. The dry, lifeless soil had caused the foundations of the house to move. Broken walls and jammed bathroom doors were what eventually led Baba to say, "That's enough." He let the landlord know he would not be renewing our lease.

❧ ❧ ❧

BY SPRING, MY PARENTS HAD found a house that Mama hated but Baba loved, so they bought it. It was in Victoria Woods, named after a queen in the hope that she would visit the area, in the Redlands, named after the clay-red earth that existed before any English queen and her colony.

As we drove into the city, we were welcomed by a long mural trailing along the main road, featuring the faces of various children. Some had crooked smiles and dark eyes. Some were bald, with heads disproportionate to their bodies. One girl had alien-like wideset eyes and an ushanka hat. She was wearing a thick black coat despite being, like all the others, set against a beach background. One small toddler sported a Hitler moustache, a recent graffitied addition. I would later find out that locals referred to this artwork as the *scary baby faces mural*. Some thought it a disastrous reflection of the city it represented. Others thought it was perfect.

Our new house was built of brick patterned with black spots, as though it had suffered a million cigarette burns. Its yellow roof had a large, inexplicable red stain on it, and sloped down dramatically, reminding me of a Neanderthal's forehead. It stood out on the road; not a single house looked like it. In the front yard was a wattle tree full of lorikeets that I would find would swoop across the main road low enough to be hit by traffic every now and again. The mailbox was shaped to look like the house.

The place was badly insulated, and excessively hot, even in spring. Baba promised to install air conditioning. It was two storeys—the first time we had stairs—but the stairs had gaps that a foot could slip right through. Baba said he would board those up. Every wall in the house was a sickly blush pink. Baba said he would paint it. "Something nice," he said. "Maybe nice modern neutral."

Mama and Baba had their own bathroom. It had an ugly mirror that looked like someone had accidentally smashed it and tried to reconstruct it there on the wall. If someone looked into it, their face would be distorted, broken into pieces. That bathroom had no door—it led straight into their bedroom. A touch of romance in the parents' retreat, the real estate agent had said. The first thing my parents did was put in a bathroom door. The lock on it worked just fine.

Whenever we ran errands back in the city, my father took the time to drive around and point out all the houses he had inspected with Mama.

"That one was nice. Very nice, but a bit dark," he says pointing to a two-storey in Holland Park. "Natural light is very important. You need natural light in a house. Of course,

NEVER LOCK YOUR DOOR | 87

your mother couldn't see that. *Add windows,* she said, as if it is easy."

Each represented a different possibility, posed a different timeline. What would have happened to my parents if we moved into the house in Mount Gravatt—the one with the beautiful kitchen benchtops but the shoddy garage? Or the house in Coorparoo that had all the natural light one could ask for, but sagging wooden floors that creaked with every step?

But they picked Victoria Woods. And that is where it all came apart.

BABA

RITA PLACES A HYPOALLERGENIC BLANKET over my father. He is sweating but cold. The powder-blue shade makes him look like a swaddled baby. He pins it down with his heavy chin. He is happy today, telling Rita about me.

"She is a writer," he says, although I've never been paid to write a word.

"I want to be. I'm not yet," I say.

"Yes, but you will be, inshallah."

Rita smiles. "You must be very proud of her," she says.

"Yes, I am. Very proud of my daughter. Inshallah, she will write stories about her father! But not about cancer." We've spoken about this before.

"No," I say, "I wouldn't write about cancer because everyone writes about cancer."

"Do they?" says Rita.

"Yes. Cancer is boring now. That's what my lecturer said."

"Cancer is very boring," says my father. "Look at us, Rita. This is so boring." He rubs his hands together underneath the blanket. "I have an idea for a book. It's about a man who works at a construction site doing risk assessment, but he is bad at it. The book is called 'Risk Ass'. Like risk assessment. But he is an ass. A dumbass." He laughs.

I ignore him. 'The best thing to write about is characters with inner conflicts. The ones who contradict themselves, and say things they don't mean, or do things they don't say. That's what we're taught."

"Well," says Rita, "that sounds very good. I will leave you two and be back to check on you soon."

I attempt to work on my assignment from the plastic chair next to my father, while he blasts the Qur'an from his phone. The other patients are either too polite or too hard of hearing to say anything.

Have we not made the earth as a bed, and the mountains as pegs? the phone sings in Arabic. I had read the lines in the Qur'an when I was a child, back when Arabic was more than squiggles on a page. My father reminds me of the lyricism of the illiterate Prophet.

"That's a nice image," I say. "It's a nice metaphor."

"You should put that in a story," he says. "The Qur'an is full of beautiful things like this. You need to read it. It is full of this." He closes his eyes for a moment. When he doesn't open them, I think he might be trying to sleep, but he smiles.

"Imagine, Soosy, 'Risk Ass'. It could be a movie. Like *Jackass*. You need to write this."

COVER YOUR EYES

THERE WAS A PERIOD OF time when Baba didn't let us watch *The Simpsons*. It came after an episode where Marge was naked, exposing her chest to Homer, although all we could see were her bare shoulders. When things he deemed inappropriate would happen on TV, he would yell, *"Ghuti wishik ya bit!"—cover your eyes, girl!*—or he'd cover my eyes with his own hand until the sinning was over. But the cartoon semi-nudity was too much. Baba turned off the TV, and we were not to watch *The Simpsons* again.

After that, we had to wait until six-thirty to turn the TV on. At six-thirty-five, on *Neighbours*, there was a scene that involved two people kissing. He turned the TV off again. His children would not be exposed to gratuitous displays of affection between people living on the same street. We couldn't watch TV until seven.

This was a shame, because I learned a lot from TV. Our family was *The Simpsons*: a bald dad, a fuzzy-haired mum and three kids. I was Lisa Simpson to a tee: middle

child, a girl, the smartest sibling—and I even had plans
to play the saxophone in the school band. Dr Karl on
Neighbours was a doctor like Mama and could cure anything, from a blocked nose to cancer, with a stethoscope.
He knew everything even remotely related to the practice of medicine, even if he did serially cheat on his
wife, Susan.

One day Ms. C, my music teacher, held band auditions in
the lunch break. As many of the aspirants had never played
an instrument before, auditions weren't so much auditions
as allocations. Ms. C would test various instruments on a
child, to see what fit best. As the brown, three-dimensional
incarnation of Lisa Simpson, I was sure I would get the
saxophone.

The students were called to the music block one by one,
in alphabetical order. Because no one could ever fully understand how my name worked, lists either had me near the top,
E, or near the bottom, *S*; it was hard to tell when I would be
called. That day was an *S* day, so I was one of the last kids. I
headed over to the music block to find Ms. C in the storage
room.

"Hello," she said. She blew upwards, as if to keep her artifi-
cially red fringe out of her eyes, even though it was nowhere
near her eyes, but cropped close to her hairline. She looked
a little sweaty as she lugged big, black instrument cases
from the back cupboard and onto the floor. "Are you ready
to audition?"

"Yes."

Ms. C smiled and pulled a piece of paper from a folder.
"Your permission form says you'll be on the levy scheme."

I wasn't exactly sure what that meant, but I knew it had something to do with my parents not being able to afford a saxophone. "Yes," I said.

"Okay. Let's get started." She unclipped a case—the smallest of the three on the floor, which held a trumpet. "There aren't a lot of choices left, but we will find you something."

Ms. C was a divorcee. I knew this because she had mentioned an ex-husband once, who was also a music teacher, working at a rival school. She never mentioned kids.

She held the trumpet mouthpiece to my face. "Blow," she said. A sputtering, flatulent sound came out.

"Purse your lips."

I wasn't sure if she wanted me to take hold of the mouthpiece myself. She pressed it hard against my face. It smelled of the mouths of a thousand children, mixed with a faint whiff of Dettol. "Harder," she said. "Now blow. Sharper. Purse your lips harder. Don't puff your cheeks out so much. Just purse."

She dropped her hand, which was flecked with spittle. "Okay. Let's try the next one." She unclipped a bigger case and picked up the mouthpiece. A baritone, a mini tuba. It was not the vision I had.

"Ms. C, could I try a saxophone? I think I'd be better at the saxophone."

"We don't have any saxophones on the levy program." She said it quickly and without looking at me.

"But I noticed the girl before me got one."

"That's her personal saxophone."

"And Adam got one too."

"Yes. They have their own saxophones. You're welcome to bring your own."

I sighed and pushed my mouth into the brass cup.

"Yes. Much better. This instrument doesn't need such tight lips. It needs big lungs, but it seems like you've got those!" She made an awkward gesture towards my chest. Was she calling me fat?

The baritone weighed a tonne and made my walk home from school a living hell. Ms. C suggested a trolley, but didn't have one to offer me. I swapped sides every two minutes to keep my arms from falling off. I decided Ms. C was a mole— I'd heard that word on *Australia's Next Top Model*—who was out to get me.

When Mama got home from work, she laughed at the noise the baritone made for two seconds before sending me to my room to practise. I practised for two minutes before Baba told me to stop.

"Can you drop me at the morning rehearsals?" I asked Baba.

"When?"

"Fridays."

"What time?"

"Seven-thirty."

"Sorry, habib. Too late for me."

"But I have to go. And Mama is working night shift."

"I have to be at the site by seven."

"Can you drop me on your way?"

"It's not on my way, ya Soos, and you cannot be at the school alone so early."

I told Ms. C I had to quit band before it had even begun. "I can't make it to rehearsal," I said. I pretended to be sad, but in all honesty, I wasn't. Band hadn't worked out how

I pictured it. I was meant to be playing on the beach in a bikini and a bandana like the woman on the *Sax on the Beach* album cover. All I was doing was lubing my baritone valves and ejecting spit onto my shoes.

"What if I pick you up?" she said. "You'd have to be ready a little earlier, but I can pick you up on the way to school. Just let your parents know."

This was a strange offer. It was hard to imagine teachers existing at all outside of school, and yet here she was offering to pick me up from my own home in her own car. I didn't know how to decline, so I said, "Okay."

The next Friday, Ms. C picked me up at six-thirty in a white RAV4. I was waiting for her outside the house because I didn't want her to get out of the car. I sat in the front because there was no door for the back. Definitely no kids, I decided.

"How are you finding the baritone?" she asked.

"It's good."

"It's a fun instrument. I thought you would like it."

"Yeah, I really like it."

We sat in silence for the rest of the ride.

When we got to school, she made me unpack the chairs and set up all the stands while she sorted through sheet music. We didn't speak a word. Maybe the only reason she offered to help me out was to get someone to do the grunt work for her.

At seven-thirty, kids started showing up. It became clear very quickly that all the pretty girls had flutes or clarinets. The fat boys had brass and, ironically, the boys who couldn't count were placed on percussion. The cool, and evidently rich, girls and boys had the saxophones. I sat in the lower brass section, next to a boy who was constantly emptying the spit valve of his trombone into the carpet.

❦ ❦ ❦

ON WEEKENDS, WE ALWAYS HAD breakfast as a family. That Saturday, I was, as usual, at the opposite end of the table to Baba and Mohamed. They liked fetta. My aversion started young, when Tom and Jerry would play with cheese that emitted dastardly stink lines. Something about those cartoons lodged in my brain, and I could not stand the stuff.

"Can I get a saxophone?" I asked Baba loudly enough to cross the distance between us.

"Eh? You already have one."

"No I don't. I have a baritone."

"*Aywa*, and it is bad."

"I don't like it."

"I don't like it either. Give it back to the school."

"So, can I have a saxophone instead?"

"No. I have a headache."

"How much is it?" said Mama, peeling a boiled egg.

"I don't know."

"Tell me how much it is, and we'll think about it."

"You can have a shush-o-phone," said Baba. "It's free."

If anyone knew how much a saxophone would be, it was Ms. C. I asked her when she picked me up the next Friday.

"They can be anywhere between a couple of hundred dollars to a couple of thousand," she said. "Aren't you happy with your baritone?"

"I am happy. Very happy. I would just like to learn the saxophone too."

Ms. C adjusted her seatbelt, which was constricting her chest. "A lot of people love the baritone. I love it. It's a great instrument." She sounded like a used car salesman. "My ex-husband plays the baritone," she said.

"Oh?"

"Yes. He's very good at it. I know if you work hard you could be very good at it too."

"Does he like it?"

"Hmm?"

"Does your husband like playing the baritone?"

"My ex-husband."

"Sorry. He must. Otherwise he wouldn't have stuck with it for so long, right?"

"It's best if you just try and stick with it. With what you've got. That's always best."

At school, I set up the chairs neatly in three rows. I had started to get a sense of who was dedicated—would show up to rehearsals—and who would just be dead weight when it came to performance nights. The saxophone section was shrinking each week. That meant there were brand-new saxophones languishing in rich kids' bedrooms, going unplayed. They'd only be carted out when parents were in the audience.

We were working on a new piece called 'Market in Marrakesh'. It sounded awful, and I had a feeling it would always sound awful. There was no way an almost all-white band of adolescents from South East Queensland could capture the essence of Marrakesh, no matter how much Ms. C tried to convince us otherwise.

We were barely eight bars in when the boy next to me in the back row emptied his spit valve onto my shoe.

"Yuck," I said. "Can you not? Ew. Stop!"

"Enough talking back there," said Ms. C from her conductor's stand, over the horrendous sound of the band.

The boy flicked his spit valve down and blocked the stream. "Is it weird having your mum at school?" It was the first time he had spoken to me.

"What?"

"Isn't Ms. C your mum?"

"No. Why would you think that? We don't look anything alike."

"You sort of do."

"We literally have different skin colours."

"I dunno. Adopted or something. Or maybe your dad is black."

"She's not my mum. She doesn't have any kids, or a husband. She has an ex, but he's not my dad."

"I said quiet back there," shouted Ms. C.

The boy emptied his spit valve again. There seemed to be an awful amount of spit, despite very little playing. It hit his leg and dribbled down into his sock. He laughed, and I couldn't help but laugh too, because he was so disgusting.

I wondered what made Ms. C's ex-husband leave her. Or maybe she left him. Maybe he couldn't have kids and she wanted them, or vice versa.

After rehearsal was finished, she called me and the boy to her office—the storage room.

"The talking today was a problem," she said.

"He was talking, not me," I said.

"I heard you. Both of you."

"She was talking about her dad," the boy said, sniggering. I knocked him on the shoulder. "No I wasn't."

"I know what you were talking about. I heard you." And then Ms. C spoke the last words I ever expected to come out of her mouth. She took a deep breath, like she was about to blow into a baritone, like she was already regretting it before she aired it, and she said, "You were talking about my boobs."

Boobs. A teacher saying the word *boobs*. Ten thousand times more strange than seeing a teacher outside of school.

I couldn't believe it. I went wide-eyed. I almost screamed.

I tried not to look at her boobs.

"What?" spluttered the boy.

"And that," she said, "is highly inappropriate."

"But ... we weren't ..." I said.

"As a female teacher, I will not tolerate—"

"This is so weird," said the boy.

"—this harassment. And that is what it is. Harassment."

"We were talking about you, but not about ... that," I said. "He thought you were my mum, and I said you don't have kids, and that your husband isn't black or my dad."

Ms. C went silent, her face whiter than usual.

"Why would we be talking about your boobs?" said the boy.

"That's enough," said Ms. C. "This is your first and only warning. Go away. Get out."

The boy and I left through the corridor.

"My sock is still wet," he said, sniggering, and I pushed him into the wall.

To say I was embarrassed would be an understatement. I was mortified, but I couldn't stop thinking about it, no matter how much I wanted to. *Boobs boobs boobs.* That's what she thought we were laughing about. She thought I was a Lilly, making fun of her chest. That moment at the swimming carnival, in that toilet cubicle, had changed the way I thought about my body. Maybe Ms. C had had something similar happen to her too. Someone had told her that her body was not okay, and she was still carrying that with her. It worried me that she was an adult and still had these feelings. It worried me, because it meant I wouldn't forget for a long time to come.

MAMA

EVERY TEA BAG ON THE supermarket shelves contains leaves that were swept off the floor in a factory in India. That's what my mother told me. She saw a documentary about it on TV. It does not matter how much you spend trying to be better than someone else, because we're actually all so scarily the same.

Every morning, when my mother gets out of bed, she takes two mugs from the kitchen cupboard. This habit is one of the few she's kept from when she was with my father. Only now the other mug is not for him, it is for me. She puts one Bushell's tea bag in each. A teaspoon of sugar in mine and an Equal in hers, and she doesn't boil the kettle until I wake up. In the meantime, she finds something to do. Like work on the chicken coop, or tend to the worm farm.

My mother has a lot of habits that keep her busy. They are not always hobbies, because hobbies imply enjoyment. Habits, in contrast, are born from compulsion. The habit of making a mug of tea for me every morning makes my sister irate. To Aisha, I am our mother's favourite, and I always have been. It is hard to disprove this, because I know I get on my mother's nerves the least of her three children.

While Aisha and Mohamed scream at each other like vultures over roadkill, I tend to keep the peace. That is, if keeping the peace means keeping quiet.

Aisha says Mohamed is Baba's favourite. I agree; Mohamed is the only boy. But, I tell her, if Mohamed weren't in the picture, or if Mohamed were a girl, Aisha would be Baba's favourite, because I look too much like Mama and he doesn't need the reminder. "You are Baba's favourite girl," I tell Aisha, but she doesn't believe me.

Mama begins to get a mug out for her too, to smooth things over. But Aisha doesn't drink tea, so the mug sits there day after day, ready with a tea bag and three sugars for my sweet little sister. So, really, Mama's habit hasn't changed at all. Every day she gets two mugs out of the kitchen cupboard, one for her and one for me. But Aisha is still not satisfied.

Aisha is a jealous type. Why, I don't know. Aisha gets everything I have, and everything she wants on top. She was luckier genetically than Mohamed and me: she doesn't have the nose. Instead, she has big doe eyes and long lashes that Mama calls cow lashes. A pretty little cow.

There is a picture of us at a school disco when I was eight. The disco was for Grade Threes and up only. I reiterated this to my parents: *Grade Threes and up only.* Aisha was not even in school yet. Not only did she demand to go, but she wore the same outfit as me—a white t-shirt with a picture of a girl on it, long black tracksuit pants and sandals. In the picture, she is in a flamenco pose, hogging the camera, and I am in the background, half shrouded in darkness, my arms extended and my lips pursed. I am trying to keep up with her.

Next to the picture in the album is a lock of blonde hair. Nana kept it from Aisha's first haircut. Aisha is Nana's favourite child. They are so alike.

BABA

THERE'S AN ARTICLE ONLINE THAT says custard apples are good for killing cancer. Baba eats one with every meal and keeps one out on the kitchen bench, in a dish of its own, at all times. He bought it when he started this round of treatment, and it is going brown and hard.

"Look," he says. "This is what it is doing to the bad cells." He holds up the rotten fruit and flicks it. It sounds hollow. "It's working," he says. "Imagine: this is my cancer before the fruit"—he holds up a fresh one—"and this is my cancer after." He drops the rotten fruit on the plate, and it clangs against the ceramic.

"You can't believe everything you read on the internet," I say. "A lot of that is fake."

He has been sharing this stuff on his Facebook page. He has also been sharing the same picture, every day, for the past three years, of a cartoon dinosaur that says, *"Rawr* means *fuck you* in dinosaur." It is accompanied by his caption, "RAWR SISI." Sisi is the new Egyptian president.

"I don't believe," he says, *"I know.* Look with your own eyes. I don't need to believe in what I can see. I can see it."

"I've seen lots of fake things online recently," I say. "I've seen articles about people who have gone to jail because of fake things they have posted about Sisi."

"That is true," he says. "He takes people's mobiles for no reason and puts them in jail. There are thousands and thousands of people in his jails right now, under the airport, everywhere. He tortures them."

"Does that make you scared?"

"Of course," he says. "But RAWR SISI."

He cuts the fresh custard apple in half and eats a spoonful. I can tell it is going down hard.

IT IS HARAM TO WASTE FOOD

NANU KAWTHER, MY PATERNAL GRANDMOTHER, wore black for the first year of my life, because her husband died one month after I was born. His first words to me were *"Akbar* Sara?"—"What's Sara's news?" He didn't have time to say much else.

Nanu Kawther died eleven years later, in Egypt. When a Muslim dies, they are buried immediately. There is no announced service, no open casket, no coffin. They are wrapped in cloth and in the ground within a day, their head facing Mecca. Brisbane to Alexandria is about twenty hours—there was no way we could've made it in time.

Nanu Kawther was a wonderful cook. Her meat was so soft it fell off the bone. Her rice was full of flavour, and she'd save me the best part—the burnt bits on the bottom of the pot, which were chewy and buttery. She burnt the rice on purpose, I knew this for sure, because whenever Mama made rice there was never as much.

Nanu Kawther's hands were small but strong. When I was young, she would take me to her bathroom after eating, cover her hands in a pungent, lemon-scented soap, and scrub my mouth clean.

Nanu Kawther was never empty-handed. When we visited her in Alexandria, she'd have already sent her house girl to get us bags of sweets from the shops. When she would come over to ours, she'd insist on stopping off at Toys and Toys before seeing us.

Nanu Kawther was from the Egyptian countryside. Her childhood friends called her Sara. She lived a content life, albeit poor, going to school and running in the fields with her friends until sunset. That's the story my father tells me. When she was eleven, she moved to Alexandria with her family and trained in sewing. She never returned to school, but she knew how to write, and she knew how to read the Qur'an. She was a deeply religious woman. The only time I saw her get really irritated—apart from when one of us didn't finish what was on our dinner plate—was when she had arguments with Nana over something the Qur'an did or did not say. She had a quiet voice that would only strain, not rise, with anger.

"Nanu" isn't an Arabic word for grandmother. It's a variation of *Nana*. When Mohamed was born, the grandparents stood in the hospital room to decide who was going to be known as what. Mama's mother bagsed *Nana*. Baba's mother wanted something similar, but with its own flavour. She tried options: *Neenee, Noono, Noona*. She settled on changing the last vowel.

Nanu Kawther did not speak English. She knew "hello" and "thank you," but other than that, when she visited us in Australia, she would just nod at people who spoke to her.

She would come every year, and each time she visited, I felt it. I was losing the language. Shame replaced warmth as I struggled to find the words to communicate with her.

In Egypt, my Arabic had been fluent. In Australia, my tongue was not cut out, but it was sanded away, gradually and painfully. My father would continue to speak to me in Arabic and I'd respond in English. You hear about people's ageing relatives losing their ability to speak, but *I* changed in front of Nanu Kawther. Her chubby-cheeked granddaughter, to whom she could once speak freely, had grown into a mute stranger. One who knew what to say, but not how to say it.

I didn't look much like Nanu Kawther, with her white skin and soft features. She wore big glasses that made her eyes look three times their size. She had straight grey hair that she'd only show to her immediate family. But she had a mole on the right side of her chin, just like me. Baba calls my mole *Nanu Kawther*, and he touches it with pinched fingers, like he's picking the essence of his mother off me. Then he kisses his fingers.

Mama collected me and my siblings from school the day Nanu Kawther passed, the last day of term. I knew something was wrong because Mama was always working and never did the school run. She told us on the way home that Nanu Kawther had died. This was the first person I'd known who had died.

"How do you know she's dead?" I asked.

"Because your uncle called," Mama said.

"How does he know she is dead?"

"She was sleeping, but she wasn't breathing."

When we got home, Baba was praying. Recently he had been praying in a chair because of his bad back, but that day he had his head pressed to the floor. I waited behind him until he was finished.

His *zebibah*, prayer bump, looked especially dark on his forehead. He hugged me and his whole body shook. It was the only time I had seen him cry.

"I'm an orphan," he said. I didn't know that adults could be orphans, but I believed him. Besides, in that moment, he didn't feel like an adult at all.

I didn't know how to act in mourning. Would I have stayed home from school if we weren't on holidays? Would I have brought it up to my friends? How would I explain that there would be no funeral? The timing made it easier to stay home and avoid the questions and guilt.

Baba went back to work and spent most of his time at home praying. I spent most of my time playing *The Sims*. I'd play until my Sims reached old age, then I'd make a new family before any of them died.

One week into the holidays, I decided it was time to do something. So I called Carly, a girl from school I would walk home with sometimes. She was a skinny blonde who always wore two braids in her hair, and was roughly the same shoe size as me. I asked her if she wanted to go shopping.

The next day, we went into Supre, where I feigned interest in buying a boob tube. Then we sat in the food court and ate Subway that tasted like soap. Then we went to a bookshop, where I found a *Sims* game guide. I'd been wanting that particular guide. It was full of codes that could give you endless cash, turn your Sims' skin purple or let them cheat death.

"Am I having dinner at your house?" said Carly.

"I don't know. I'd have to ask my mum."

"Because I told my mum I was having dinner at your house."

"My house isn't the greatest place to be at the moment."

She looked up. "Why?"

"Because everyone is sad. My grandma died."

"Nana died?"

"No. My other grandma. My dad's mum."

"Oh. I didn't know you had another grandma."

"Well, she's dead now."

"Oh. Sorry." She looked down to her hands, and I kept my eyes on the shelves. "Can I still come over for dinner?"

Mama made *bamya* stew, meat and rice. Carly sat in my usual seat, and I had to drag a garden chair inside and perch on the corner of the table. I only ever did that—gave up my seat—when Nanu Kawther was there. Baba was quiet at the dinner table; he preferred silence when eating, especially at the moment. His left arm stayed anchored to his placemat, while his right lifted food to his mouth, or waved to beckon a plate. He smelled of the sour citrus cologne he showered himself in every day. He reached across the table and grabbed the pot of rice, digging out two spoons for himself, then two spoons for me. In it were the dark, chewy, buttery bits. Mama must have done that on purpose.

Carly ate her rice and bits of meat, but left most of the bamya and sauce on her plate. She was a picky eater, she said. The only time I'd seen her be a picky eater was when she picked her nose at school.

"Is your friend going to finish her food?" said Baba. He said it with a smile, so as not to scare Carly. He had found at work that people often misinterpreted his tone, called him aggressive when he was just loud and plain-spoken.

"Are you going to finish your food?" I repeated to Carly.

"I don't think so. I'm full."

"There is not much left," said Baba, even though there was a lot left. "Yalla, Mama, finish your plate." *Mama* is what adults call little girls in Egypt—it's a term of endearment. Like when they call them *aroosa*, doll. Or a bride.

"I don't think I can," said Carly.

"Yalla, Mama, it is haram to waste food."

"What does that mean?"

"If you do haram things," I explained, "you will go to hell when you die. Go on, eat it. Or my dad will be mad and you will go to hell."

"Shush! That's not a nice way to speak to your friend," said Mama. She wasn't in her usual seat either. She always sat next to Baba, but she had swapped with Mohamed to sit on the other end of the table, and that's where she stayed from then on.

Baba and I kept our eyes on Carly. She started to sniffle. Of all the people at that table who had reason to cry, Carly was the one to do it.

MAMA

WHEN THE SMELL OF CARAMEL fills the house, I know my mother is waxing. She doesn't like shaving, or the chemical removal foams. Hot sugar is different. It's a more natural, healthy burn. An earthy one.

The sugar my mother is melting on the stove smells good enough to eat, but it is not for eating. *Halawa*, that's what it's called. Sweet. She asks me if I want some, and I say no.

When it's caramelised, she pours it onto baking paper. She waits a little, allowing it to form into a cohesive blob. She keeps most of it in the fridge for next time, when she will get it out and knead the hardened sugar over the fire.

More often than not, a razor is my tool of choice. I would rather cut myself than have my skin ripped from my under-arm. My mother is a tough woman. She can withstand anything.

She shows me and Aisha how to use the halawa properly. This is not the first time she has shown me, but I still can't get it right. Last time I tried it, I ended up sticking myself to the carpet by the crotch.

Aisha does it. She is not afraid of pain. I am the weakest member of this family. Last time, my whimpering could be heard throughout the house.

My mother pulls up her pajama pant leg and places a small bit of caramel. I can see her blue varicose veins.

"I gave her those," Aisha says about the veins, in a tone approaching pride.

Then, in a quick movement, Mama strips the halawa off her leg.

"If it weren't for you," I say to Aisha, "Mama would have nice smooth legs. She wouldn't have any problems."

"I don't ever want to have kids," says Aisha. "They're a waste of money and they give you varicose veins."

"That's true," says Mama. "But if you don't have kids, then what's the point? What will be your legacy?"

"Lots and lots of money," says Aisha, grinning.

RULE NO. 9

LIFE IS NOT A FAIRYTALE

I HEARD THAT ALLAH MADE man out of mud. Fetid mud. Makes me wonder what was wrong with a nice piece of wood, or a rock. Stinky mud. That's us. Putrid mounds rolling across the earth, thinking there's something more to come for us.

My gut rolled over my naked thighs as I sat on Carly's toilet. It wasn't the first time it occurred to me that I couldn't see my crotch when I sat. Just three rolls, rising over one another, as if they were racing to reach my knees and the bottom one was winning. Allah used a lot of mud on me. He didn't have to, but He did.

There was a knock at the door.

"Are you okay?" called Carly. I had been in there for a while.

"Yeah. Just finishing up." Fetid. A smell. Soaking my underwear. Trickling down the toilet bowl. Pooling on the floor. I knew I couldn't hide in there forever.

❧ ❧ ❧

THIS IS HOW I GOT THERE. Spring Fever: the end-of-year show at school. Every year, each grade would put on a performance across a three-night extravaganza. The main event was always the Grade Sevens, who performed an extended musical act, usually based on a Disney movie. It was the highlight of the year. Everyone looked forward to it, and it was finally our turn.

The Grade Sevens gathered in the hall on a Friday afternoon. It was February, and the sweat under our twelve-year-old armpits stank of impending puberty. The acoustics meant the whir of the industrial fan above us, spinning at full speed, was drowned out by our chatter.

There were rumours the theme would be Snow White. I struggled to think which part I could play. The lead would be, for obvious reasons, out of the question. And I was too tall to be one of the seven dwarves. The past year had seen me grow taller than almost every kid at school. I knew it wouldn't stay that way for long—Mama had assured me of this. We were a short family. But for now, it counted against a starring role.

Ms. C was wearing a halterneck, which sat so close to her throat it must have been itchy. She raised one hand in the air—a signal for us to quieten. The boys in the back row continued to whisper, although they were listening. We were all listening. We all wanted to know.

Ms. C ran a finger under her tight collar, as though to give herself some air. Then, she spoke. "You all know that Spring Fever is a privilege. Yes? We don't have to do this. If you are not on your best behaviour, we will cancel your performance. All right?" She had everyone's attention now, and she knew it. "With that being said. Our theme this year will be *Aladdin*."

She didn't look at me when she said it, but I felt like she was talking to me. Just me. She had chosen this theme with me in mind. I couldn't believe my luck. *Aladdin* was as Arab as you could hope for.

"You've got Jasmine for sure," said Carly as we left the hall. "You're the only one who looks like her." She was right. I was the only kid in school remotely like Princess Jasmine. I had Jasmine's nose, Jasmine's eyebrows, Jasmine's ambiguously Islamic background. It didn't matter that I wasn't dainty. This role was made for me.

Our class began to practise every afternoon. The scene with Aladdin being chased by guards for stealing a loaf of bread would open the show. Carly was placed in front because she was short, and she had started doing jazz ballet, so she could at least hold a kind of rhythm with her feet.

Ms. C pretended she was giving everyone an equal chance at the lead roles. Watching us as we learned the moves. Praising those who picked them up quickly. Until the leads were cast, Ms. C said, we needed a stand-in, to block Aladdin's movements. She tapped me on the shoulder. I had to run and jump over boxes as three boys, playing the guards, chased after me. The rest of the class danced in the background. I could see Carly out of the corner of my eye, looking at me and grinning. Ms. C was prepping me. Was she wanting me to be the star? I had nothing against it, but my heart was set on Jasmine. She had to know that.

The next Friday, the announcement came.

"You've all done well to pick up the dances," Ms. C said. I knew she was being generous. Half the kids in my class couldn't sway on beat if their life depended on it.

Ms. C slid her finger under her collar again before she spoke. "Our Aladdin... will be Jake."

This came as a relief. Jake, one of the tallest boys in the grade—one of the few taller than me—smiled at his friends, restless with excitement around him. Ms. C must have thought carefully about her choice, I thought. Jake did not look Arab at all, but he would make me look smaller by comparison. I would make a good Jasmine next to him.

"Settle down, please, boys," said Ms. C. "Now, our Jasmine."

I grabbed Carly's hand and jiggled it in excitement. When Ms. C announced it, reading off her slip of paper, all the girls sitting in front of me turned around and looked. Those big, fake, jealous smiles on their faces. But they weren't looking at me. They were looking to my right. Carly. Ms. C had said Carly.

I listened to the rest of the list. The Genie. Abu the monkey. The Sultan. The bad genie. Jafar. Jafar's parrot. None of those roles went to me. I was to be in the background.

❧ ❧ ❧

LATER THAT WEEK, CARLY INVITED me to her house after school. Perhaps this was her way of apologising. We hadn't talked about it, the possibility that I wouldn't get the role of Princess Jasmine. But something about the way she didn't look me in the eye when I said *congratulations* made me think she knew. There were dynamics at work that I was too naive to appreciate.

Although she'd been over to my house countless times, I'd never been to hers. She said that she liked our house better, that was why.

I knew that we lived in the same neighbourhood—her house was just a little further away from school than mine,

I imagined. It was spitting when we started walking, but it was raining solidly by the time we passed my house. We kept going. Past the park with the fossilised dirty nappy sitting proudly in the bark. Past the big traffic lights. Past the smaller park with the rust-encrusted swing set. We walked for what seemed like ages, until we turned into a big driveway, lined by trees. I never realised Carly lived this far away.

Two cars sat in front of a double garage door. The house was light grey on the outside, and all white on the inside. Even the couches were white. They screamed to be soiled.

Both her parents were home. Business owners, she had once vaguely mentioned.

"Why do you walk home from school if your parents are here?" I asked, drying my face on the inside of my collar.

Carly shrugged.

"Because she insists on walking with you!" called her mother, who had overheard from somewhere in the depths of the house. She emerged and didn't introduce herself, but smiled at me as she took our schoolbags from us. "I'm putting these on the patio to dry." This didn't make a whole lot of sense to me, but then I realised their patio must have a roof.

There was a plate of fairy bread on the kitchen bench, already buttered and perfectly sprinkled. On the dining table was a blue midriff costume. Her mum had been hand-sewing rhinestones onto it.

"She's more excited than I am," said Carly. "I don't really think I can do it."

"Nonsense!" said her mum as she came back inside. The woman had good hearing. "Everyone on the P&C agreed you'd be a great Jasmine."

Pee and See. I didn't know what that meant. Like peeing in the toilet and then checking the colour. Pee and See. I was reminded that I had been holding on for a while.

The sliding door that led onto their backyard opened, and in came a large man with a salt-and-pepper moustache. "So many bloody toads out there," he said, shaking off the wet. "Bloody unnatural buggers." He was holding a golf club with a streak of what looked like blood on it. He didn't seem to see me sitting at his kitchen bench.

"Eww, gross, Dad," said Carly. "We're going to practise." On the way to her bedroom, we passed a closed door, metal music emanating at low volume from behind it. Carly had an older brother, in Mohamed's grade. I'd seen him at school before they graduated primary, but had never spoken a word to him. I realised I had forgotten his name.

Carly's room was at the back of the house. It was huge. She had a big bed, with enough room to spare that we could dance and not bump into anything.

I had been watching Carly and Jake, as everyone was forced to, during rehearsals. I was only in one number, but Carly was in at least six.

"I really can't keep track of all the routines," she said. I knew she was just saying that to make me feel better, as if being a star was a burden that I was lucky to dodge. But I had already learned all her steps by heart. We both pretended I was doing her a favour by standing in for Jake.

The lifts were easy, because Carly wasn't that big. I could do it better than Jake as I wasn't afraid to touch her in the wrong place. I lifted her in the air as she jumped. Twirled her and dipped her.

Carly asked if I would like to swap. "Maybe you can be Jasmine for a bit," she said.

"Why?"

"It'll help me learn the moves, backwards and forwards."

I knew she was doing it for my sake, but I didn't care. She stood on her tiptoes as I bent my knees and twirled under her arm. I braced my weight as we went in for the dip. Tightening my bladder with every eight count. I needed to go, but I held it in. Just to maintain the feeling of doing a dance made for me.

Then came the lift. There was no hiding that she couldn't pick me up. I jumped, pretending someone would catch me. But I landed with a thud, straight back on my own two feet.

"Maybe they just needed someone who could do the lifts," she said, sympathy in her voice.

"Where's your bathroom?" I asked. Urgency in mine.

Carly took me down a corridor which seemed to last forever. The walls were covered in framed photographs of her—those staged glamour shots where the photographers make pre-teens look like middle-aged women by adding thick burgundy lipstick. A smell of vanilla wafted from a candle that didn't look like it had ever been lit.

The bathroom was, again, all white, except for the gold fixtures—on the shower, the sink, the bath. Beside the toilet was a wicker basket filled with fresh paper rolls, signifying plenty, like in a magazine spread. Another virgin candle sat on a narrow table nearby. This one smelled of coconut. The whole experience was distracting enough for me not to notice one critical feature of that bathroom. The toilet seat. The lid was down.

Once I realised, it was too late. I was peeing *on* Carly's toilet. The piss ran down the basin and onto the floor, pooling near the wicker basket. I had peed on Carly's floor. I panicked and threw an entire fresh roll into the puddle to soak it up.

I tried to stop myself, but I couldn't. I stood, still going, and lifted the lid. The urine on the back trickled down into the joins of the toilet.

When I finished, I took stock of the damage. My skort was soaked. I removed it, swishing it around the floor with my foot in an attempt to wipe up the mess. It was no use. It was a lost cause, and so was I.

I slumped on the toilet. Looking at my stomach. What a lot of mud Allah had used. Adding and adding, layer by layer. All for the ignominy of being looked at with disdain while covered in piss. My stomach was not the stomach of Princess Jasmine. It would not fit into the pretty midriff laid out on that dining table. And it was not very princessy to piss oneself, even in a grand bathroom. The role wasn't for me. It never was. Allah didn't make me for that.

As I pulled up my wet skort, squeezed it tight to remove the excess and buttoned it over my stomach, I decided that there was no point in pretending. I wiped up what I could. I opened the door.

On the way home, a cane toad sat in the middle of the road, where it had been soaking up the rain. Its eyes glowed an almost pretty yellow. I watched as headlights approached and a car came into view, leaving a splatter of guts in its wake.

The rain had stopped. There was nothing to explain away why I was wet.

BABA

BABA SAYS THERE IS A nice boy he wants me to meet. He
brings it up when he knows he has got me: as we enter the
supermarket. I can't make a scene, and we came in one car,
so I can't escape. He brings a picture up on his phone. He's
already friended the boy on Facebook. This is the third he
has found. I walk ahead of him because I don't want to talk
about it.

My father cleans the trolley handle with an alcohol wipe.
His reduced immunity concerns him most when he sees
snotty-nosed kids in public spaces. He doesn't try to catch
up to me because he knows I will wait for him, always.

"He works at a chemist," he says, when we are in Fresh
Produce. He asks me to find a good avocado. I squeeze until
one gives a little under my thumb. It is in its prime.

I am careful not to say anything that will entertain the
idea of me *getting to know* a complete stranger just because
he is Muslim. "Baba, I don't think I would get along with a
pharmacist. I'm not into that sort of thing."

"No, no. He is not a pharmacist. He works at a chemist."

We avoid the brown bananas. My father is picky enough
to pass over the yellow bananas too. He likes green bananas,

because they will keep in his house as long as possible. This is despite the fact that he leaves them to go brown anyway. He saves them with the intent of making banana bread, even though he lacks a recipe.

"Just get to know him, just as friends," says my father.

I want to ask when it became okay to be friends with boys, but I know the answer to that. "Where do you find these people?" I ask instead.

"He lives in Sydney. He is my friend."

"*Is* he?"

"His father is my friend."

"Really?"

"Yes. My Facebook friend. Just get to know the boy. Okay? As a friend. That's it."

"I already have enough friends."

My father is unhappy with the bananas I've picked out. He removes them from the trolley and chooses a bunch that looks almost identical. He pulls out an alcohol wipe and cleans his hands. He says he wants a grandchild before he dies. He's been saying this for years, but I don't find it funny anymore.

❧ ❧ ❧ RULE NO. 10 ❧ ❧ ❧

NO FIGHTING WITH YOUR BROTHER

I FIRST LEARNED THE WORD *fuck* from Mohamed. We had only just arrived in Australia, and I was watching *Hi-5*, counting down using different combinations of my stubby little fingers. *One, two, three, four… Hi-5.* One combination left, my middle finger last in the air. Mohamed told me that meant something rude.

"What?" I asked.

"Don't say it," said Mama to Mohamed, watching from the couch.

Mohamed came close to me, leant over and whispered, "It starts with *f* and rhymes with *duck*." I said it out loud and Mama smacked him hard on the back of his curly black head.

"Ibn el kelb," she muttered.

Another word you were not supposed to say out loud was the c-word. They called it the c-word at school because it

122

NO FIGHTING WITH YOUR BROTHER | 123

was the dirtiest word imaginable. They said things like *dick* and *cock* and *knob* all the time, but apparently they were not as dirty as the c-word.

I don't remember when I learned the word in English. I do remember, though, learning it in Arabic. We hardly ever had couscous at our house. When Mama made it for dinner, I said, "Thanks for the cous, Mama," and she hit me in the back of the head. Mohamed leant over and whispered what *cous* meant in Arabic. Mama came back to wallop his head too.

When Mohamed was thirteen, he punched his first hole in the wall. The wall, in the hallway of our house, was an olive colour. It was worse than the blush pink it covered.

Mohamed punched the wall after fighting with Baba, and he left afterward. I figured Mohamed had wanted to punch Baba but was too scared. When Mohamed punched the wall, he must have had a lot of words he wasn't supposed to say in his head.

Mohamed had a guitar on his bedroom wall. This wall also had a hole in it, from opening his bedroom door with too much gusto. The guitar was an acoustic that my parents had bought for him. He had defaced it with a Sharpie: drawn flowers and, in big curvy letters, the word *breathe*. Of all the words he could have written, he chose *breathe*.

When Mohamed was fourteen, he took his first punch to the nose. It was spring 2007 and I was standing up on my bike, riding as fast as I could, and screaming. A magpie, an angry one, was tailing me. She wanted me dead. I rode across the street, not looking where I was going. My shoe-lace had come untied and was the hitting the wheel with a *clang clang clang* that let me know that at any moment it could get caught in the gears. I was shouting for someone to help me. People drove by but they didn't stop. One man slowed, only to flash a smile and then drive on. I started to cry. I didn't know where Mohamed was; he had sped ahead. The blows to my helmet, the screeching so close to my ear, were too much to bear. The magpie swooped, clicking and squawking as it clawed at me.

My bike was new, a present from Nana. It was black with orange and red flames, and graffiti-style writing on the frame that read SPEED. I had picked it to impress boys. Which boys, I wasn't so sure. The only boys I hung out with were my brother and his friend Nick. I was only allowed to hang out with Nick when Mohamed was there. Nick was a haemophiliac and his mother didn't let him ride bikes, so it was just me and Mohamed out on the two-wheelers.

I didn't like Nick very much. He had a crewcut that showed the sweat pimples on his neck, and would ask me if I had a boyfriend every time he'd see me.

"Hey. Mohamed's sister. Come here," he'd said the last time he was over at our house. He always called me "Mohamed's sister," as if it would have been uncool to actually learn my name.

"I don't have a boyfriend," I said.

"No, come here. I have a secret to tell you." He leant over and cupped my ear with one hand. Then, in a quick movement, he slurped on one of his fingers and stuck it in my ear. For a boy whose blood didn't clot, he had a lot of nerve.

I'd heard that magpies swooped people to protect their babies. They see humans with shiny things as a threat.

That magpie was determined to see me go down. I was scared, and I was mad that not a single person stopped to help me. The bird followed me, screeching, hitting my helmet with its beak with every swoop. The sound reverberated in my head. I ducked, too scared to look at it for fear it would take my eye out.

I looked ahead and saw Mohamed standing on the footpath ahead of me. His bike was lying on the ground, and he was staring at the fence of a stranger's house.

"It's going to kill me!" I yelled. "Help!"

As I got closer, I could see that Mohamed wasn't looking at the fence, but what was sitting on it. A magpie sat still on the wooden planks, staring back at my brother.

"Kill it!" I yelled.

"I stopped and it left me alone," he said, not taking his eyes off the bird. He was still. Just staring at it, making eye contact in a moment of calm that betrayed the difference between us. I barrelled past, my assailant bashing my head in the whole way home.

There was no more riding bikes after that. This meant I had to walk to school.

Carly—who remained my friend despite my mishap—would walk home with me. Aisha, in Grade Two, would trail us, sucking on a warm apple Pop Top like a teat. Carly's favourite thing to talk about was the sealed section in *Dolly* called Dolly Doctor. Opened by a thin strip of perforated paper, it was filled with secret confessions. She'd read the letters to me as we walked.

"This one is called 'Wormy Problem,'" she said. "*For the past two years or so, I have noticed that when I poo there are little white things in there that move. Does this mean I have worms?*"

"Ew."

"Okay. What about this one? *Is it possible to catch A-I-D-S from a public swimming pool?*" She stopped and looked at me. "What is A-I-D-S?"

I shrugged.

She shrugged too, and continued. *"My mum won't let me go to the local pool because she says she is certain I will catch A-I-D-S, but I don't think she is right. Is she?"*

"Next," I said.

Nana was cooking when Aisha and I got home. I grabbed a Zooper Dooper from the freezer and sat outside. On summer days it was too hot to sit anywhere else. Our yard consisted of a large concrete slab that covered half the lawn. This was intended to be a future patio, but the patio part never happened, so we just had half a yard of concrete. The house would provide enough shade on the concrete in the afternoons to make it habitable. The Zooper Dooper wrapper cut into the edges of my mouth.

Nana called out that there was someone on the phone for me.

It was Carly. "Hey, is your brother okay?"

"Why?" I asked.

"My brother said he was in a fight."

"What? With who?"

"I don't know. He just said there was a big fight at school."

The knob clicked and the front door opened. Mohamed came in, dropped his school bag and headed to the kitchen. His back was sweaty.

"He just got home," I said into the phone.

"Who are you talking to?" Mohamed said. I heard the freezer open and shut.

"Carly."

"Who's Carly?"

"My friend."

"Did you eat the last Zooper Dooper?"

"I have to go," I said to Carly, and hung up the phone.

I stuffed the wrapper into my skort pocket.

Mohamed was leaning on the kitchen bench, chewing loudly as he ate a banana. He had a way of clamping his teeth together when he chewed that really pissed me off.

"Stop," I said.

"Stop what?" he said.

"The chewing."

"I'm eating. There's nothing in the house and you took the last Zooper Dooper."

"Stop arguing," said Nana, peeling potatoes over the sink.

"You can eat without chewing so loudly. And I didn't take the last Zooper Dooper." As a kind of karmic punishment for the lie, I felt the last bits of syrup in the wrapper drip into my pocket.

He threw the banana skin in the bin. There was a reddish-brown line running down the front of his school shirt. "What's that?" I asked.

"Bird poo," he said, without looking down. A little was crusted on his upper lip.

"Did you eat it, too?"

Mohamed wiped at his nose. He left the kitchen, heading for his room.

I pulled the Zooper Dooper wrapper from my pocket and stuck it in the bin, flicking Mohamed's discarded banana skin over it to hide the evidence. Underneath the skin I saw a piece of scrunched yellow paper that looked like a permission slip. I went to the bathroom to wash "my hands.

"Hey." Mohamed appeared again, wearing a fresh t-shirt.

"What?"

"Do you know how to use the washing machine?" He was holding his school shirt, crumpled into a ball, in his hand.

The next day I waited until I knew Carly had left before I started walking home. I didn't want to talk about what had happened.

The walk home seemed longer without Dolly Doctor in my ear. Aisha and I reached the intersection where our road met the school road, and I saw a magpie, dead on the grass near the gutter. There were often dead possums here—the exposed wire that ran along the telephone line above got them. As soon as one possum corpse disintegrated into dust, a fresh, plump corpse would appear on top of it. It was the circle of life. This, however, was the first time I had seen a magpie here. Aisha winced at the sight of it and hid behind me as we walked past.

The phone was ringing again when we got home, and I ignored it.

"Can you answer that, Soosy?" called Nana from the kitchen.

I ignored her too.

Aisha picked up the receiver. She listened for a moment.

I already knew who it was. "I don't want to talk," I mimed.

"She doesn't want to talk," said Aisha into the phone, then said to me, "Carly says why?"

"Tell her because I feel sick," I said.

"She said she feels sick. Okay. Bye." Aisha hung up.

Mohamed was unusually late. He didn't get home until almost five o'clock. He dumped his bag and went to the kitchen, and I followed him. His shirt was clean this time.

"Where were you?" I asked. I didn't expect a straight answer.

"At school," he said into the fridge.

"All this time?"

"Yah."

"Were you in detention?"

He didn't look at me. The fridge started to beep. It had been open too long. "Hmm," he said.

"Why?"

"Cuz I was standing near a fight and got hit by accident. Why do you care?"

"Can you close the fridge? That sound is annoying."

I tried to imagine what it would look like, Mohamed fighting someone. I'd never seen him hurt anything but a wall. Mama had told me that when I was a baby and Mohamed was two, I was crying and Mohamed grabbed me by the scruff and held me under his arm. While I was still screaming, he dragged me by my neck across the house. He stopped at Mama's feet. "Baby cy-ing," he said.

Mama lost it, thinking he had hurt me. But he had been gentle. He just wanted to let her know that I was upset.

Mohamed and I didn't speak for the rest of the evening.

He went to his room and I could hear him fire up his Xbox.

I wasn't sure if Mama and Baba knew about the detention. They did not bring it up when they got home, but we were not the type of family to discuss these things. Not when it came to my brother.

I decided not to say anything. We ate Nana's food, and everyone except Mohamed returned to the living room. We watched the first five minutes of *The Simpsons* before Baba changed the channel to the Arabic news.

The phone rang again.

"Soos, go get it," said Baba.

I reluctantly got up. "Hello?"

"Hey. Are you okay?"

Carly. Again.

"Why wouldn't I be?"

"Aisha said you were sick."

"Yeah. I am sick."

"What kind of sick?"

"What do you mean?"

"Are you head sick? Tummy sick? Too sick to come in to school tomorrow sick?"

"I don't—"

"*Period* sick?"

"What? No."

"Diarrhea sick? Are you shitting yourself?"

"Jesus, Carly, shut up."

"*Aeeb ya*, Soos. Don't speak like that," said Mama from the living room.

"I'm just sick, okay?"

"Okay," said Carly. "How is your brother? Did he do his detention?"

"How did you know he had detention?"

"My brother told me."

"Your brother is nosy."

She was silent for a moment. "Being nosy is better than being aggressive."

"Who is aggressive? I'm not aggressive."

"Your brother is. He was in a fight."

"He was watching the fight and he got hit accidentally. That's different."

"Well, my brother said your brother punched someone because they called him a bad word, and then they punched him back."

"What did they call him?" I wondered if I would need Mohamed to translate this bad word, as with cous.

I could hear Carly cup the phone as she whispered, "They called him a Muslim."

I laughed. "That's not a bad word. Do you mean a terrorist?"

"Yeah, sorry. Terrorist. They called him a terrorist. My bad."

For just a second, I wished I could reach through the phone and punch that girl right in the nose.

BABA

MY FATHER ASKS ME WHAT I think the problem is with Mama. I am sitting in his La-Z-Boy. It is stuck and won't recline, but it rocks, and that is comfortable enough for me. Each rock is a little squeaky, which I am sure gets on his nerves, but I keep doing it.

I tell him there is no problem anymore. My mother asked for the divorce years ago. We were all there, we all saw it. And it is done. It is time to move on.

He says he never understood what went wrong. He has said this before.

"Does it matter?" I say. "Does it really matter? Aren't you happy now?"

I ask because I know, in a way, he is. But he looks tired. Despite his condition, he wakes up at four every morning to pray, and does not sleep until midnight.

"Will you ask her for me?" he says.

"I don't know what you want me to ask. It's been a long time."

"And can you imagine I still don't know?" I have irritated him. "Stop rocking."

I realise I have been rocking pretty fast. It is easy to lose myself in the comfort of the rhythm. I move over to a static dining chair. This is where my father sits every morning to pray. On the table in front of me is a pillbox that looks full of Skittles; a *sibha*, prayer beads; and a plate with a digestive on it. I was, for a time, obsessed with digestives, the chocolate-coated ones. I'd go through boxes. Now I can't stand the sight of them.

I don't have to look at my father to feel sorry for him. His sadness is in this chair. There is a collage on the wall that Aisha made him for his birthday. It is carefully curated with old family photos that do not include my mother, in a hope that they will not remind my father of who was behind the camera. We hope he can accept that now there is only him and us. At times, he can.

My father says he's asked a friend of his, a doctor, what he thinks of the situation.

"There is no situation," I say.

"He said she must have some mental health." He means mental illness. "Maybe something is wrong, you know, in her brain. That is what he thinks, and he is a doctor. Because no one would act like this for no reason. For what reason? I am only saying this because I am worried. So you need to ask her."

I don't say anything because I don't know where to start. I take the digestive and bite it because my mouth needs the distraction. It is familiar and wheaty—too familiar. I spit it out onto the plate.

"Eh da?" says my father. "What is this? Haram." He clicks his tongue and I wipe my mouth.

NO ONE LIKES SURPRISES

THE CEILING FAN IN THE dining room was on high. Its blades blurred into one, whirring extraterrestrially around a still centre. There was no air conditioning in the house yet. The hot food made it worse, but there was no such thing as a cold dinner in our family. Regardless, there were no complaints, because the dinner table was for eating, not for talking. If we were talking, then we weren't eating, and if we were eating, we showed our gratitude by shutting our mouths.

But Mama didn't follow this rule. Not that day.

"I have a question," she said. The little food she had taken on her plate—a bit of red sauce on potato, soft meat—sat untouched. She sounded odd. Almost as if she was nervous.

Baba didn't look up from his plate, but everyone else did. Baba didn't seem at all surprised by the departure from routine. The fan blew the few hairs on the top of his head as he kept his eyes anywhere but his wife.

"A question for who?" said Mohamed. He was holding his fork like a shovel. This irritated Nana, who always reminded us of dining etiquette. Backs up straight. Elbows off the table. I could see it in her face—she was about to tell him off.

"For whom," said Nana. *"It's a question for whom."*

"For everyone," said Mama. She wasn't holding her knife, but she was rubbing the silver handle with her index finger.

"Mohamed," said Nana. "Fork."

"What? I'm eating," he said.

To understand the gravity of the question Mama asked us, I need to explain what occurred a few weeks before—Open Day 2007 at Victoria Woods State High School. Primary school was coming to an end, and everyone went to Open Day to get a taste of what high school would be like. Of course, the school put out all the good bits. The Home Economics block offered free samples of smoked salmon on Jatz with cream cheese. Neon posters of girls in hotpants dancing on stages were plastered all over the Performing Arts building. Dance was the school's biggest drawcard. But inside, standing between the barefoot dance girls and the drama kids in socks, was what I considered the best attraction: James Stickler.

There was something about James Stickler that made me want to commit, body and soul, to him. We had first met two years earlier, when he was in Grade Eight and I was in Grade Five. We were brought together by Immersion Day, designed to encourage primary-school kids to continue with their instrument practice—an attempt to convince us that we shouldn't abandon our brass or our woodwind or our poor lip control, but nurture it, even if it meant confirming our own social doom. To convince us that it was indeed a good idea to keep lugging around that degraded piece of sweaty metal. To keep pretending we could read treble clef.

We were about to take a deep dive into the waters of wind orchestra and puberty. Our primary-school band would be combined with the high-schoolers, and we would play with them at a special concert later that evening.

James Stickler was the only person I had ever met who played the same instrument as me, the baritone. And that was enough. I was immediately obsessed with his four-eyed face. Five eyes, if the pimple in the middle of his forehead was counted.

We shared a stand and sheet music during rehearsal, an intimacy which to me was akin to sharing a lovechild. The piece was "A Disney Spectacular"—a medley of movie themes. Ms. H, the high-school instrumental music teacher, was doing an admirable job concealing her disgust at the sound coming from the group as she conducted us.

James Stickler and I had eight bars rest while the others played the intro to "Be Our Guest." James turned to me and said, "Be natural."

My cheeks went a little hot. "What do you mean?" I said. I thought he had caught on to my nervousness.

"B natural. Not B flat." He hit the sheet music with his finger. "You're missing the accidental on the B. It sounds weird."

But here James was again, in a room smelling conspicuously of foot odour, looking a little older. He was taller and his hair was shorter than when I had last seen him. I liked his hair longer. He still had a pimple, in the very same spot—a testament to his persistently greasy skin, accentuated by a widow's peak that I hadn't noticed before. I approached him, smiling just enough for him to think I was being friendly, but not too much in case he had no memory of me. He smiled back.

"Are you interested in joining band?" he said. His voice wasn't what I expected. Something must have dropped.

James offered me a brochure, printed on yellow paper. It felt warm, as though he had been holding it in his hand for a while. I wanted to ask if he remembered me, but before I could, I was interrupted.

"Do you guys have guitars here?" said a voice from behind me. I turned and saw a boy in a uniform I didn't recognise. One of the other feeder primary schools the high school was trying to recruit from.

"Yep," said James.

"Sick," said the boy, and took a brochure.

The truth was, I didn't need James to sell me anything. I was already sold. I'd been sold for years. There was never a doubt in my mind about which high school I would go to. It was Victoria Woods or bust. And my parents agreed, in the sense that they did not give me a choice. They would never pay for schooling because, compared to Egypt, any school was private here, and there was no point in paying thousands of dollars a year just to learn a little more about Jesus.

Carly was also going to Victoria Woods. She followed me around the various stands. She picked up every brochure, including the music one, even though she had never been in band. She wasn't in anything.

"Since when do you care about band?" I asked.

"I dunno. Maybe I'll learn something new next year," she said.

"You can't learn something new in high school."

"Why not?"

I didn't have an answer, but I decided I would make new friends in high school.

"Is that the boy you were talking about?" she said. A framed picture hung on the wall of the Performing Arts block as we exited. It was of the jazz band. James was in it, and he was holding a trombone, not a baritone. He was branching out, and I needed to as well.

"Yeah."

"I thought you said he was cute."

Carly had no taste.

❧ ❧ ❧

THOSE HOLIDAYS WERE FULL OF hot rain and bad sleeps. Dreams of yellow brochures and older boyfriends. I would never be going back to primary school, and that was a good thing. My uniform was soiled with signatures from people I didn't think of as friends—who never really were friends—but who signed my shirt in exchange for me filling up space on theirs. We held on to our faux popularity like a branch in muddy waters. Throughout the summer we'd hear of people up north getting hit by cyclones and we'd curse the storms for the residuals of rain they'd send and the skyrocketing price of bananas. Bananas we didn't realise were still in our schoolbags, left in December, discovered in January, bruised, beaten and black.

❧ ❧ ❧

THIS IS THE QUESTION MAMA asked at the table: "How would everyone feel if I worked in Maryborough for a little while?"

She said it, and then picked up her fork and started to eat.

I had never heard of Maryborough. "It's where the lady who wrote Mary Poppins was born," she said, with her mouth full.

"Julie Andrews?" said Nana. "Oh, I love her."

"No. Not played Mary Poppins. Wrote it. The lady who wrote the book."

"What? In England?" I said.

"No, Mama, you can't go to England!" cried Aisha. Aisha was at the irritating age of seven, where she was young enough to want Mama with her all the time, but old enough to hit me in the face in a way that really hurt.

Mama laughed. "No, not that far. It's just a little north from here."

"Oh? She's Australian?" said Nana.

"Why do you want to work there?" said Mohamed.

"I don't want to, I have to. I have to do hours in a regional area so I can finish my studies. It's been too long. This is a way they let me speed it up." She was talking about the practical hours she had to complete so she could qualify as a doctor in Australia. None of us really understood what *regional* meant, other than existing in some other region, in some other place. Where we lived was regional to us. Baba understood what it really meant, though, because Mama had explained it to him already. It meant somewhere far away.

"If that's where you want to go," said Mohamed, "then why are you asking us?"

"It's not where I *want* to go," she said. "But would you be okay with that?"

Baba, still silent, got up and took his plate to the kitchen.

"I suppose it wouldn't make much of a difference to you," said Mama. "You could stay here. But it would mean I would live somewhere else for a while."

"No!" said Aisha. She was about to cry.

"Now, I've looked it up and Maryborough looks a bit old. The clinic is there, but I think I will find a place to live in Hervey Bay instead. It's right next door to Maryborough. It's a bay. A beach. It's nice," said Mama.

"I thought you said it's a little north from here?" I said.

"It is. Four hours north." Mama got up and put the lid on the pot of rice.

"But you can't do that," I said.

"I have to."

"If you have to, then why did you ask?"

"Well, my question is, actually, would you stay here, or would you want to come with me?"

"No," I said immediately.

"For how long?" said Mohamed.

"A year."

'When?"

"Starting in January."

"But I can't," I said. "I'm going to Victoria Woods."

"You don't have to come with me."

"I've planned everything. At Victoria Woods."

"That's okay," said Mama. "You don't have to come. You can stay with your father."

Baba was in the living room. The TV was already on.

Aisha piped up. "I'm going with you," she said.

Mohamed swallowed his mouthful, finally. "I'll think about it," he said. He liked to pretend he was in control, so he said that even though he was as stunned as I was. Even though it changed nothing.

Mama stacked Mohamed's plate onto hers, then Aisha's.

Victoria Woods was High School. Anywhere else was impossible to imagine. Barren. Regional. Far away and non-existent. There were people waiting for me at Victoria Woods: James, even Carly. I had the brochures. I had the uniform.

"But I won't have any friends. How do you expect me to survive high school without friends?" I said. It's at that point a parent is supposed to say, *you'll make friends*. But Mama wasn't making any promises.

"Think about it," was all she said.

I hated that she was giving me a choice, even though she knew my mind was already made up. I tried to imagine my life next year. Going to Victoria Woods, being with James and Carly. Living in a house without my mother, and only my father.

Mama took my plate. I hadn't eaten much, but she knew I was finished.

That's when it came loose. There was a loud crash. I instinctively shut my eyes. When I opened them, shards of opaque glass were all over the table. I looked up and saw the bulb in the fan was exposed. The fan continued to whirl without its missing part.

Aisha screamed. Mohamed laughed. I began to cry.

❧ ❧ ❧ RULE NO. 12 ❧ ❧ ❧

PETS ARE NOT PERMITTED

ASBESTOS MANOR WAS A TWO-STOREY house on the Esplanade in Hervey Bay. I didn't make up the name—nailed to the front deck of the house, which was painted entirely in Sunshine Yellow, was a slat of wood with the words imprinted. It was hard to miss.

"Who the hell lives there?" said Mohamed.

We passed it on the way to our new place—the place we would call home for the next year. The car was packed to the brim: our duvets pressed against the back windshield, Mohamed's toes pressed against the front. The buttons controlling the windows were smeared with remnants of KFC. Aisha was squashed between Nana and me in the back seat. Our knees were scrunched up to our chins, our necks sore from the four-hour trip from the Redlands. Mama was driving, focusing on the GPS and actively ignoring us. "Paper Planes" by M.I.A. blasted through the earphones of my MP3 player. But it wasn't enough to drown out their voices.

"Probably a drug dealer," said Aisha. I assumed she had learned about criminals from Nana's *Sopranos* binge sessions.

Nana wouldn't let Aisha watch with her, but I'd seen Aisha sitting in front of the TV from time to time and Nana's head flopped down to her chest in a deep doze, the sound of Tony Soprano yelling amid sleep apnea–induced gasps.

"Why would a drug dealer live in a bright yellow house? Are you stupid?" said Mohamed.

"You're stupid."

"You're the dumbest person on earth if you think a drug dealer would live in a bright yellow house."

I caught a glimpse of the sign hammered into the lawn outside Asbestos Manor. FOR SALE: $5,000,000. I imagined the person who lived inside had a grudge. An old and long one. Or was completely delusional. Welcome to Hervey Bay.

Our townhouse was relatively new and had no rumours of asbestos, as far as we were aware—not that we asked. It shared a wall with neighbours we didn't care to meet because we weren't staying long. There were three bedrooms: this divided up as Mama in one, Mohamed in one, Nana and me sharing one, and Aisha on a trundle bed in the living room. There wasn't enough room for Baba if he wanted to visit, because Mama had claimed the master, and they hadn't been sleeping in the same bed for a long time.

Mama's main gripe about the place was that the kitchen was upstairs. This made it hard to carry shopping from the car to the fridge. But we'd have to live with it for a little while.

Mohamed set up his fish tank in the living room. Both were modest: the tank could hold about five small fish of different colours and shapes; the living room could fit a couch, a TV and a trundle bed. Some fish in the tank were pretty enough, but there were two little ugly brown ones that would suck on the glass. They had a parasitic look about them. I couldn't tell if they were enjoying themselves or wanted out.

Fish were the only pets we were allowed to have. No matter how hard we had campaigned, Baba had never allowed us to get a dog, as he said it would disqualify his prayer; dogs were considered dirty, and one has to be clean to pray, so having a dog in the house would mean his prayers weren't valid. But Mama said the real reason was that Baba had had a bad experience with a dog in his youth. Now Baba wasn't living with us, but still no dogs—the place was a rental, Mama said, shaking her head.

❧ ❧ ❧

ON THE FIRST DAY OF school, Mama took the morning off work to take us. The air had a scent that reminded me of when we first came to Australia—a combination of heat and sweat. Mama never took time off work unless absolutely necessary, especially now that she had to keep up with Hervey Bay rent on top of her part of the Victoria Woods mortgage. For her to take the time to drive us to school must have meant that she felt sorry for us.

A sea of kids in red polos flooded through the gates of Fraser State High. I didn't want to join them, but I had to. I followed Mohamed, who didn't seem phased by the change of scenery. This was the first time in two years I had been at the same school as my brother. I had finally caught up to him in high school. Being in the same school usually meant living in the shadow of his reputation. It wasn't that he was super clever or set particularly high standards, it just meant I was always referred to as Mohamed's Sister. But this was a new place, where neither of us was known. It might be a chance for us to have each other's backs for once.

"You have to go to your area," he said, destroying my illusions of fraternity immediately.

"What area?" I said.

"Your class."

"Where is that?"

"I don't know. Look at your timetable."

I assumed my timetable had been sent to Mama, if I had one. Maybe somehow, in the feverishness of moving, Mama had forgotten to tell me I needed to make a schedule. The email could have gone to her junk folder. Or maybe she thought I was smart enough to figure it out on my own.

Before I knew it, Mohamed had disappeared.

Nausea crept up on me. I saw a kid whose shirt looked bright enough to be new, like mine, and followed him. He was weedy-looking, with brown floppy hair and skinny arms.

At first glance, the place was just like primary school—the open walkways, the demountables, the leopard trees sprinkling leaves all over the footpaths. But the feel was different. A girl who also had a bright red shirt on walked by, smelling like cigarettes and looking as though she had somewhere to be. I thought about smiling at her, but I felt too intimidated. A group of boys stood near a set of tall water bubblers; one was shoving his friend's face into a tap as he took a drink, and the clang made my own teeth hurt. They laughed it off, the victim holding his mouth with one hand, adjusting his gel-smothered hair with the other.

We ended up at a tin-clad hall that doubled as a basketball court. The kid I was following obviously knew something

I did not. Once the bell rang, students were ushered into lines inside the hall. Everyone seemed to know which class they belonged to. I felt like I was missing something.

I sat down next to the boy. A teacher at the front of the hall shushed into the microphone—a long, loud shush that caused a squeal of feedback, until we all suffered from tinnitus. The teacher spoke of suspensions. Someone had set a kid's hair on fire on the bus. The school year had been running for less than three minutes and already there were suspensions.

The weedy boy next to me was making soft but audible gasps, in between picking bits of gravel out of his sole and throwing them at his friend, a well-built redhead down the row.

He was eventually successful at getting his friend's attention. The redhead turned and made eye contact with me. He looked annoyed, but then I saw he was holding back a laugh.

I sat in his smile for a moment. It was the first flash of familiarity I'd experienced since arriving in the town, even though I was aware it wasn't for me. The weedy boy pointed to the girl sitting in front of him. He put his hands to his own head and wiggled his fingers, grinning at his friend. I followed his gaze, and my jaw dropped involuntarily. You could actually see them—hundreds of little brown lice running around her hair like ants in a disrupted nest. I backed away, into the kid behind me. "Sorry," I whispered, without looking at him. He didn't say anything. I imagined him frowning at the back of my head. The redhead made a face that was a combination of amusement and disgust. *Fucking yuck*, he mouthed to his friend, but I pretended it was to me, and smiled at the joke.

After assembly, I was pulled up by a teacher who was quietly taking attendance of her class. She sent me to the office, where a timetable was printed out for me.

I did not say a word for the rest of the morning, other than "here" when a teacher took the roll. In each class I picked a seat that had a view of the clock. The seconds moved slowly.

Mohamed was nowhere to be found at lunchtime. I had thought I would be able to scan the grounds and see his fuzzy black mop, but it was just a blur of red shirts, flat hair and unfamiliar faces. I looked for the weedy boy. I looked for the redhead. I even looked for the lice girl. I gave up, settling on a patch of grass in direct sun, while others gathered in the shade in friendship groups already formed, carried over from primary school. The grass itched the backs of my thighs, and the sun was giving me a headache, but I didn't get up. I was already too tired.

After school, everyone gathered at the front gate. Multiple buses pulled up, set to disperse to different suburbs across Hervey Bay. I peered at each, looking for the one to our area. I clutched my pass, ready to go.

Mohamed sauntered to the gate with what looked like a new friend. It bothered me, how easy he found it to make friends. He had his shirtsleeves rolled up, just like the boy with him. He stopped a few metres away, chatting. I could have walked over and stood with him, but I couldn't get my legs to move. Having to explain who I was to Mohamed's new friend or, alternatively, just standing next to Mohamed in silence and not introducing myself: both prospects seemed dreadful. The group of boys I saw that morning near the bubblers were now running around laughing, shooting a staple gun at each other. One copped it to the arm; the other suffered a staple lodged in his forehead. If that was what it took to fit in at Fraser, I didn't have it in me.

The bus finally arrived, and we shuffled on. I sat in the front, so I could watch for familiar landmarks and get off as soon as we reached our stop. The girl who smelled like cigarettes boarded and sat across the aisle from me. Her skirt was rolled up, half its original length, and she was sporting black eyeliner. She played "Low" by Flo Rida loudly on her flip phone. I looked around. No one seemed bold enough to stop her. Not even the bus driver. I wished I had her confidence. I put my earphones in but didn't play anything. I didn't know how I would survive a whole year in this place.

That evening, I spent a long time in the shower. I lathered, rinsed and repeated. Over and over and over. Afterwards, I made Mama check my scalp for lice.

❦ ❦ ❦

MAMA WAS NEVER AN AVID prayer, but once we moved, she started doing all five daily prayers. She got up at around four am to pray fajr in the living room. If she placed herself correctly, she could face Mecca perfectly *and* see the horizon through the kitchen window. I think she hated the kitchen a little less in those early hours of the morning.

I was taught to pray according to a routine. You stand while you say one part. You bow at the waist for the next bit, and then you go to your knees for the last. You have to recite different things in each position. Once you're finished, you start again. The number of repetitions depends on the time of day. But sometimes, when I'd watch Mama pray, she'd spend a long time on her knees, her forehead pressed to the carpet. People tend to spend more time like this when they have lots of questions, or need extra help. On one morning, Mama said she heard a loud crack, as if of a glass pane, while she was bowing. She looked up at the window; it was fine. The sun was just starting to come through, turning the sky from black to purple. She looked around the room and saw Aisha still asleep in the trundle. At first, she thought she was hearing things. But then she felt something at her knees. She looked down. Water pooled in the carpet.

It was the fish tank. A large crack ran across the glass where the ugly little brown fish had once sucked. They were now convulsing in death throes on the carpet. When Mohamed woke up, he screamed and wept into the floor.

🐾 🐾 🐾

EVERY SECOND WEEKEND, WE WOULD fold into the car and drive back to Brisbane to visit Baba. It would've been easier, I thought, for him to visit us, seeing as we were five and he was one. But it was the way it was for some reason. Every fortnight was a reminder of where we would return to eventually. That this diversion from normal family life was temporary.

I was looking forward to this trip because Baba had told me he had got Foxtel.

We passed Asbestos Manor on our way out of Hervey Bay. The blinds were open, and I tried to see inside, but it was too dark. There was washing on the line, so someone was living there. A king in an asbestos castle.

"They were ugly anyway," said Aisha. "No one liked those fish."

"You're ugly," said Mohamed.

"I think we're lucky, in a way," said Mama. "You don't often get the chance for a clean new start. New house. New fish. Looking forward to the future. Forgetting everything else."

"I'm not getting new fish," said Mohamed. "I'm never having fish again."

BABA

THERE IS A CAT THAT visits my father's house every day. Her grey hair is soft and fluffy, like a fur duster. She has a belly that sags. A primordial pouch. I've read about them on the internet; it's to protect their internal organs. My father doesn't let her into the house, but he talks to her through the flyscreen. She paws at the mesh, sticking a claw or two in at times, threatening to rip. I know this irritates my father because he doesn't like his things being ruined. He tells her, "I don't have food for you, habibi." It makes me happy when he uses the word *habibi*, because it means he's not upset, rather that he feels sorry for her.

He loves her—he's told me so. But at the same time, he's scared of her. I don't think he's afraid she will hurt him. He is scared that she will get used to him, reliant, and he will not know how to take care of her. This cat is his companion, more consistent in presence than me. Sometimes she greets him at the back of the house, sometimes at the driveway as he pulls in. She is not skinny enough to be a stray, but it's unclear who she belongs to. She scales all fences, pledging allegiance to no one.

I ask my father if I can give her something to eat, but he says no, because if I do she will keep coming back. But she does that anyway.

My brother turns up at Baba's house around dinnertime. He seems to have a sixth sense for when food is ready. Supersonic hearing for the sound of a hot plate hitting a table. The speed with which he pulls into the driveway always scares me; I worry the cat is there. But he hasn't hit her yet.

He springs into the room. Once he's finished eating, he sits on his phone streaming UFC, guffawing at every takedown, and then leaves. I feel I have more of an obligation to my father. Perhaps I am making up pre-emptively for all the ways I will disappoint him in the future. I sense Aisha has this feeling too. She does the dishes and puts his clothes in the dryer.

Mohamed could punch my father in the face one day and bend to receive a kiss on his forehead the next. Sometimes he doesn't answer Baba's calls for weeks. I pick up on the second ring. Baba describes Mohamed as *ghalbaan*, which means poor, or helpless. He's not aware of his behaviour. He doesn't mean any harm. So Baba lets it slide.

There is some *Zuan* in the fridge, my father says. Chicken spam. I retrieve it and cut it into small pieces, and take it outside to the cat. She's still there, rubbing her cheeks against the CrimSafe. I place the spam on the ground, on a napkin. She puts her nose to it and sniffs, but doesn't eat it. This is frustrating, because it took a lot for me to convince my father that I could give her food. She meows at me, and I say, *what do you want?* She lets me pat her, then meows again. She walks to the end of the patio, and I follow. She looks behind as she walks, as if to check I'm still there. We reach the back fence. The sun is setting and the sky is a brilliant red. I want to take a picture but my phone is inside—by the time I get it, the sun will be gone. So I stay and take it in. It's like watching fire.

The cat meows, then jumps onto the fence. I feel as though she wants to show me something. Her belly swings as she jumps again and disappears.

Inside, my father is standing, looking out the window at the dying sunset. He is saying something in Arabic to himself, and I only catch a few words. It's a thanks to Allah. I know his heart is hurt, but it is opening.

KEEP YOURSELF INTACT

IT WAS A NEW FEELING, blacking out—ears blocking and vision disappearing but for a few sporadic splashes of light. I shuffled out of the classroom like a zombie, unsure if I was heading in the right direction. I ran into the side of the door, pinching my shoulder in the hinge, then into a cement column outside. If it weren't for the excruciating pain and the impending void of darkness, I would have considered being embarrassed.

This is how it started: I was in Year Eight Science. The teacher asked the class to gather around the projector screen so he could show us a video about koalas. We were studying environmental science, which at the time meant watching reruns of Steve Irwin programs. Steve was weighing a baby koala to make sure it was developing properly. I started to feel faint just as I watched the joey climb onto Steve's head and nestle into his hair. I often got dizzy spells now. Since moving to Hervey Bay, I had lost a lot of weight—not intentionally. But this was more than vertigo. This felt like a power down. The joey's name was Berry, and that's the last thing I remember hearing before I started to lose my senses.

"Excuse me, sir," I said. "Can I go to the bathroom?"

The teacher should have known something was up, because I didn't make eye contact. I didn't look at anything, because I could hardly see anything. I couldn't hear his response, and I wasn't sure he had even heard my question, but I turned around and headed for the door anyway. I made it to the closest bathroom, hoping each step would land, but as I tried to enter the toilet block, I hit a cage door. The bathroom was locked. I felt as though Allah was testing me. Either that, or he really wanted to see me ruin myself.

I could feel my stomach turning as though one of Irwin's saltwater crocodiles was inside me, its scute grating at my uterine walls. I managed to make my way to the toilets near the school office. I busted the stall door wide, pulled my pants down and sat. As I saw the stream of dark blood enter the bowl, I buckled over. This wasn't my first period, but ever since I had started losing weight, my periods had become more and more painful. I was sweating profusely even while I was shaking. There was rising bile in my stomach. I gagged, and it made it as far as my throat, only to slip back down again. My leg jittered involuntarily.

I spoke to Allah then, for the first time in years. I told him that if he wanted to kill me in that moment, I would be okay with it. Anything to get me away from the pain.

An hour passed before someone came looking for me.

A voice called out into the bathroom, "Sara, are you there?"

It was Tamara. She and I had gotten to know each other a little on the bus. I thought she was cool. She never offered me one of her cigarettes, because cigarettes were expensive, but she had said if I ever got some she would teach me how to do it.

"Yes." I spat onto the floor. The bile again. "I'm in here."

"Are you okay?"

"No. Is my bag still at the science block?"

"Not sure. Do you want me to go get it for you?"

"I just need a pad."

"Oh, hang on." Tamara shuffled in her bag and handed me something thin under the door. The pink packaging was damaged, and I could see the tampon inside. I swallowed, and took it so as not to be rude.

"Thanks," I said.

I had never used a tampon, and I wasn't about to start with Tamara outside the door. The only other time I had seen one was in Grade Five, when the school put on "Girl's Night" for mothers and their daughters, sponsored by U by Kotex. That ordeal was worse than the sex ed course we had been subjected to weeks earlier—then we had watched a video that featured a cartoon penis that looked like a poinciana seedpod, but at least parents weren't present. At Kotex's night of nights I had to sit next to Mama while a lady in a pantsuit described the smell of discharge. The only saving grace was that we were each given a gift bag when we left, full of feminine hygiene products. The cute prints on the wrappers made me excited to start bleeding. Mama took the bag, removed the tampons, and gave it back to me.

"Why can't I have those?" I said.

"Because those are not for girls."

Tamara brought me my bag, in which I found a fresh maxi pad. She took me to the office, and Mama was called. Mama couldn't leave work, so Nana was called. Nana asked whether I could be sent home in a taxi. The answer was no. Nana picked me up in a taxi. Aisha was with her too.

"If I have to pay a two-way fare I might as well make the most of it," Nana said when I asked why Aisha got an early mark because I was sick. "What have you eaten today?" she added as I remained semi-conscious, still clinging to my stomach.

"Nothing. I didn't feel hungry."

"Well, that's why you're sick. You need to eat something. You look terrible. So pale. Do you get any sun at school? You look awful."

"It's because I have my thingy." I was ashamed to use the word *period*.

It was novel to be home on a weekday. The bay air was vibrant when the weekend crowds weren't around. I tried to get some sun on the balcony, but there was only its warm memory left on the tiles. I lay on the tiles for a moment, face down. This soothed the pain in my stomach a little. The glass door opened, and Nana emerged with a pack of Advil, a glass of water and a banana. I took the Advil and the water.

"I don't want to eat that," I said.

"Then what do you want?"

"Are there any raspberries?"

I was addicted to frozen raspberries. Some days it was all I ate. I didn't like them fresh, or thawed. They had to be in our freezer for a couple of days—the whacked-out temperature setting caused them to form into hard blocks of ice.

I'd sit in front of the television or my computer, or stand at the freezer door, fingers cold and red, and crunch through the ice to the sweetness within. Mama told me about a thing called pica where people with low iron and low blood pressure tend to eat strange things. But I was there for the raspberries, not the ice.

I took a warm shower after eating. I was the thinnest I had ever been. My hair looked puffy around my drawn face. In actuality, I was losing hair by the clump. I could feel it running down my legs in the shower. I put the shower head on my stomach. The warm water helped the pain. I could see myself in the reflection of the shower door. I looked small. Young. Like a child, the girl who was made fun of for her nipples all those years ago. But I didn't hate my body. In fact, I actually liked it. I liked the way my rib bones jutted out, and I liked the way my arms were so thin I could fit into clothes I wore as a nine-year-old.

❦ ❦ ❦

THE GRADE EIGHTS WERE THE last to go on break at the end of the year. All the older grades went on holidays as soon and their exams ended, but we were stuck in the oppressive heat until the last possible moment. As a consolation, the teachers organised an end-of-year treat for us. We had a choice: either an excursion to the beach or a trip to the cinema to see *Twilight*. I had bought a bikini at Big W the last time I was there. I kept it stashed away in my room, and would try it on in the bathroom. It was deep blue with black trimming. I liked the way my body looked in it, especially the way the drawstrings tied neatly atop my hip bones. Tamara and I agreed to take the beach option.

When I got to school, Tamara was already there, waiting for me near the toilets.

"Do you need to change?" she asked me. I shook my head, pulling the strap of my bikini from underneath my shirt to show her. She smiled. "Just give me a sec," she said. She disappeared into the toilet block and I followed. Although I hadn't eaten or drunk anything that morning, I went into a cubicle anyway. I unbuttoned my skirt. The feeling of being able to use the toilet without removing a one-piece was elating. I felt free. I felt normal. What could Lilly say if she saw me now?

"Come on," called Tamara. "I'm waiting outside." Her shadow passed my cubicle.

Then I saw it. In the crotch of my bikini bottoms was a dark blotch. I couldn't know what it was for sure, I told myself. It could just be a discolouration in the fabric. I touched it. My fingers came back red. I pulled at the toilet paper dispenser and wiped. More red. Sure enough, this was Allah punishing me for the bikini, I thought. It had to be.

I had brought underwear to change into after swimming. I took my bikini bottoms off and stuffed them in my bag. There was no pad in the front pocket, where one usually lived, just an open, empty wrapper. I cursed myself for being too lazy to replace it. Toilet paper would have to do. I wrapped some around the crotch of my underwear and stuffed some more into my bag. I knew it wouldn't last long.

When I emerged, Tamara was still waiting outside.

"Took your time," she said.

Already the cramps were coming on. "Do you have an Advil?" I asked.

She reached in her bag and fished out a loose turquoise capsule.

"A pad too, by any chance?"

"Bad luck," she said. She reached in again and pulled out a tampon. "You can swim with this, at least."

"I don't know how to use it," I said.

She looked at me strangely, like she didn't believe me. But she turned around and went back into the toilet block. Inside the cubicle, she mimed what to do. "You can put your leg up on the toilet. That might help if this is the first time. You just have to try and find where it fits."

I pulled the wrapper off the tampon. Its shape was intimidating. I felt like I was doing something unnatural.

"Do you want me to leave or stay?" said Tamara.

"I don't think I can use this," I said.

Tamara looked disappointed. "It's not that hard," she said.

"No, it's just that…" I paused. "I'm not allowed to use them."

"Why not?"

"It'll break my hymen. Like sex. I'm not allowed to do that. Not until I'm married. Or my parents will kill me."

Tamara laughed. "This is nothing like sex. Trust me." She took the tampon out of my hand. The words *trust me* lingered.

"Do you want to go to the movie instead of the beach then?"

"No. I'll come with you. I just won't swim."

Minutes later, I could already see the back of Tamara's neck burning as we sat on the beach. She had insisted that we sit in the sun, to tan. She hadn't applied any sunscreen, even though it looked like she needed it. At least some of her was protected: she was wearing a bikini too, but hadn't taken her skirt off yet.

"So, when do you leave again?" she asked me. She had asked me before. I didn't know if she was forgetful, or just checking that the plans had not changed.

"In a couple of weeks," I said. As much as I had wanted to be at Victoria Woods, that afternoon, sitting on the sand at Hervey Bay with Tamara, wasn't so bad.

A group from our class were playfighting in the water: two skinny girls sat atop two boys' shoulders, squealing as they flailed around, grabbing at each other's wrists. "You can go in," I said. "I'm fine here."

"I don't really feel like it," said Tamara. She was a lone wolf; that much was clear to me from the first day I saw her. But I wondered whether it was always by choice. She twirled a twig in her fingertips, like it was a cigarette.

"I would do that with you," I said, nodding to the game in the water. "Could be fun."

"Yeah, I don't really want your period on my neck, thanks."

We both laughed.

"How about I just stand in the water. Below crotch level."

"All right," she said. She got up and dusted the sand from her backside, then pulled her skirt down. High up, near the tops of her thighs, were faint lines. Some looked like stretch-marks. A few were deeper, still fresh.

She turned around and headed for the water. I watched her dip her foot in. She walked in, the water rising to her shin, then her knee, then covering her scars. I meant to follow her, but I didn't. And she didn't turn around. Tamara was used to being on her own, I told myself. But that didn't make leaving any easier.

USE YOUR WORDS

WHEN WE MOVED BACK TO the Redlands, things were different. My parents started sleeping in the same room again. We were able to convince them to get us a cat. Her name was Mama, and she was a grey tabby. She only gained that name because she fell pregnant before we could decide what to call her. Mama Cat's baby daddy was a stray Manx that lived in our neighbourhood. Ginger and matted, he had been lurking around the street for at least the last eight years and, judging by the network of ginger cats in the neighbourhood, enjoyed a free-love lifestyle. Chaz. That's what Baba named him, because his face reminded him of a philandering tradie he used to work with.

I hadn't been inside a mosque since my days at Morningside. The last time I went, Baba had talked to the old Pakistani imam. They spoke in English, because the imam only used Arabic when reciting the Qur'an. He had turned to me and asked if I understood what he had said during prayers. I nodded, because I was too embarrassed to admit that I had no clue. I knew the prayers by heart, but I didn't exactly know what they meant.

"*Allahu la ilaha illa hu,*" he said. "*Al hayyu l-qayyoom.*"

I stared back blankly.

He looked pleased with himself, making a young girl feel ashamed for praying in a language she did not understand. I felt like asking him a question in Arabic. I could've said a swear in front of him, like cous, and he would never have known. But I knew that would be bad. The next time Baba asked me to go to the mosque, I refused.

Perhaps Baba thought after I returned from Hervey Bay that I had spent enough time in self-imposed exile, that I needed to get back in touch with my faith. So he dragged me along with him one Sunday afternoon. We pulled up in front of the mosque, an old, boxy building that was past its salad days. The imam had the keys and would only open the doors at prayer times. It used to keep much the same hours as a 7-Eleven: the devout were able to walk in and speak to Allah any time they liked. But then Molotovs, bags of dog shit and homemade pyrotechnics seemed to find their way through the doors too. Disgruntled neighbours who didn't think the mosque belonged left gifts. So now we had to wait for the imam. Occasionally, Baba said, graffiti would appear on the outer walls, or a pig's head would arrive at the doorstep, but inside was safe enough.

I told Baba I had forgotten to bring a scarf with me, so I couldn't go in. He didn't say anything—he knew there wasn't much he could say to convince me. He got out of the car without a word and made his way inside. I watched a group of hijabi women walk in. They were all chatting in Arabic.

I listened hard; it sounded like the Lebanese dialect. To me, Lebanese Arabic is like pig Latin: the words are jumbled, but if I listen hard enough I can decode them. But they were speaking too fast, with too much excitement in their voices, for me to catch on.

Something compelled me to follow those women. The way they were speaking made me curious; perhaps I could understand if I tried a little harder. There was an old towel sitting on the back seat of Baba's car. It looked nice enough to be a scarf. I grabbed it and put it over my head, draping the ends around my neck. Even if someone were to see me in it, they wouldn't know me. The perks of being estranged from the community.

I reached the door and looked inside. I could see Baba kneeling near the front. The women were at the back, still chatting. Prayer hadn't begun yet. The imam—a younger man I had never seen before—was sitting on a plastic chair in the corner. In front of him was a girl in hijab; an older man, who looked like the girl's father; and a white man, who looked lost. I could hear bits of what the imam was saying. He was talking about hadiths. There are two major parts of Islam, he explained. First there are the words. These are recorded in the Qur'an. They are the words of God, as passed through the Prophet. The second is the practice, otherwise known as hadith. Hadith is not the direct and explicit word of God, but the practices of Islam as observed and recorded by Prophet Muhammad's peers. Some hadiths are widely accepted. Some are widely disputed. It's hard to know the difference. Each imam will likely tell you a different story. He was telling the man the basics.

The girl sitting next to the white man looked embarrassed, but the white man was listening intently. It looked like she had brought in a non-Muslim who wanted to convert for marriage. A part of me felt jealous of her, while another part felt sorry for her.

After a little while, the imam shook the white man's hand and excused himself. The father of the girl joined the floor, kneeling near where Baba was. The girl joined the group of women at the back. And the white man came towards the door. I let him pass, but he didn't go much further than where I was standing. He waited there, just outside. The imam began leading the prayer as the group behind him followed his movements. I couldn't join in, even if I wanted to. I had forgotten what to say. I stayed at the door and watched, and once it was over, I went back to the car.

When Baba returned, he spotted the towel in my lap.

"What you doing with that?" he asked, before taking it to wipe the sweat from his head and throwing it into the back seat. We sat in the car for a few minutes, the engine running.

"I helped build this mosque," he said. He told me, not for the first time, of the tile work he had designed for the internal archway. "I was on the site one day, and they were planning on making it just a plain old wall," Baba said. "But it is the house of Allah, so it has to be beautiful. I started drawing a pattern that I thought would look nice. I took my time. I was drawing on the wall in pencil. I didn't finish it. I left it there. The next day the imam called me and said, 'Hey. That design you did. Can you come and make it happen? We'll pay you ten dollars an hour.'"

I scoffed. "What a rip-off."

"I would have done it for free, Soos. It is the house of Allah. But yes. Ten dollars an hour."

I would never do that. Not for anyone. Not even for Allah. I could never be as good a person as he was.

He reached over my lap and opened the glove box. Inside was a small transparent packet, carrying a thin gold chain. He handed it to me.

"While you and your mother were gone, I did some cleaning in the house," he said. "I found a lot of Nanu Kawther's old things. There was some gold jewellery. I knew you would not wear it. So I took it to be melted, and asked that they make this." I pulled the chain out of the packet. A square pendant swung from it, inscribed with a stylised Arabic word I couldn't make out.

"What does it say?" I asked.

"Allah."

Shame crept up on me. Of all the words, I should've been able to recognise *Allah*.

"I didn't melt everything," he said. "There is one thing she told me to save for you. It is a bracelet. A very beautiful gold bracelet. You can't get anything like that here. Not Egyptian gold like that."

"Where is it?"

"She told me to give it to you when you get married. When you start your legacy."

۞ ۞ ۞

ON MY FIRST DAY BACK, Victoria Woods High seemed different from how I remembered it.

"It's like you're returned from the dead," said Carly. I may have been resurrected, but she was reincarnated. She had dyed her hair burgundy, and was much taller than a year earlier. She spoke differently, too. She used words like "considered" and "forming," as in the sentence "Have you considered forming any new friendships here?" She sounded like our guidance counsellor. Part of me thought she was a sellout. Part of me thought maybe I had been the one holding her back from being her best self.

In the brochures, which still sat on my old bedroom desk, Victoria Woods High was a place where kids tucked in ironed shirts beneath uniform jumpers and gold ribbons. In reality, it was also a place where students, from time to time, stabbed each other clean through the hand with etching tools in art class. Or pile-drove a rival into the ground outside the library before the morning bell. It was a place where teachers hoped for the best but expected the worst. Sometimes they got the best—Victoria Woods bred the most competitive dance troupes in South East Queensland, the smartest kids in the country when it came to Science and Engineering Tech. Carly told me she was in the academic class.

I rejoined band, thinking that playing the baritone again may help me to reconnect. James Stickler was in Grade Twelve, due to graduate that year. But the spark I once had for him was now long gone. I had lost the dream. Victoria Woods wasn't anything like what I wanted it to be. All I could think about, as I went through the motions each day, was how much I missed being with Tamara. I found myself wondering if she was okay. I texted her for the first couple of weeks of school, but she slowly stopped replying. She was used to being alone, I reminded myself. It was time to move on.

A month into the school year, in the biggest move in the history of the Victoria Woods instrumental music program,

Ms. H announced that the band and the choir would be attending the Tutti Youth Music Festival. Schools all around the world would gather in Beijing to attend masterclasses and put on a musical spectacular. Ms. H said it would be a once-in-a-lifetime chance, and I, being the only baritone player, was invited. It was an opportunity, I thought, to get away, even for a little while. At every moment I made myself feel alone. Even if I had Carly in my ear. I wanted to be far away from it, and China would do. There was an old book in the library: *Mandarin 101*. I checked it out.

I told Mama about the trip, and she told me to ask Baba. It would count as the longest time spent away from my family—that is, if I didn't include the year away from Baba. I knew it would take a lot to convince him to let me go.

Asking him for something always started the same way. "Inshallah," he would say.

Mama Cat brushed up against my legs as I stood before him in the living room, trying to convince him to let me travel to the other side of the world. Mama Cat was a timid thing, startled by loud noises. So when all of a sudden Baba boomed, "Why are you so interested to learn another language when you have let go of your mother tongue?" she jumped and tried to hide under the couch. She got stuck halfway, her pregnant belly too big to slip under. Her back legs stuck out, like those of the Wicked Witch of the East under that house.

I didn't have an answer to Baba's question. He was right: every word I spoke to him in English was proof that I was a failure. A disappointment to my language, my religion and my family.

When I asked him again a week later, he reluctantly agreed to let me go, on the condition that it would be my birthday present for the next decade. He was showing his kindness, because he knew I had been sad since I returned from Hervey Bay.

I knew my parents were unhappy too, as much as they tried to hide it. Baba would sit in front of the television every evening and talk about how he was thinking of leaving his job. Baba's troubles at work often stemmed from his struggles to get people to understand his intentions. It wasn't his fault; English was his second language. People would take his words, and when they didn't fully understand them, make new meanings for them.

Mama would listen, then she would get up and make tea. She'd make Baba's strong, despite Baba liking it pale. The thought to spit in it even crossed her mind—the look on her face told me so. I wasn't sure at what point my mother started to hate my father, but it was now well behind us. Every word from his mouth seemed to boil her blood. I don't think there was a specific catalyst, a flick of the switch. That would have been simple to explain. If he had done something awful, like beat her, that would have been easy to understand. But he wasn't that type of man. This hatred was gradual. Brewing slowly, and with depth, like the kind of tea Baba had asked for.

❧ ❧ ❧

IT WAS A SUNNY DAY, but my parents had the curtains in their bedroom closed, as if that would block out their voices too. Mama called me in, saying they wanted to talk to me. I sat on the bed. A crocheted picture of a flower, a gift from the receptionist at Mama's work, hung on the wall. The flower's edges were jagged, unnatural. Mama hadn't hung it up when we were in Hervey Bay, but she had hung it up here. It looked like we were back for good.

"Your father has some news," said Mama. Her face was hard to read.

"Yes," said Baba. "We're moving to Cairns." The words sounded strange coming from his mouth, as though he had picked the wrong sentence. We had only just moved back; we couldn't possibly be leaving again.

Or that's what I was supposed to say, as a teenager who needed stability. *I don't want to move schools again. I don't want to leave my friends.*

But I quite liked the idea. I wanted to get out of Victoria Woods.

"Your father got a new job," said Mama.

I saw the way he was looking at her, carefully, as though they had rehearsed what they were going to say and he was making sure his lines came out right.

"For how long?" I said.

"What do you mean, *how long*?" He was angry that I'd asked. "Forever. A job means forever."

My mother was looking at me like she was trying to tell me something. They hadn't asked to speak to us kids together. Mama had called me in only. She did that on purpose. I was sad in this place, but I could see she was much more so. Her sadness wasn't grounded in a place, like mine was, that she could leave behind at the end of a day. Her sadness was in that room, and she was stuck there. I was her ace to play, and I knew what she wanted of me.

"But I can't go," I said.

"It's not your decision to make," said Baba.

"But we've already paid the deposit for my trip."

"What trip?"

"Her China trip," said Mama. I had said the right thing. "We can't get that money back."

"So you think a school trip is more important than your husband?"

"Did I say that?" said Mama. "I said we paid money, and we will lose it."

"I don't want to move schools again," I lied. "I really want to go on this trip."

"So how come you moved for your mother and not for me? How come you move so easily for her and not when I tell you?"

"I wasn't moving forever," said Mama.

"Why do you feel okay to disrespect my decisions and not hers?"

"How about you go and try this new job for a couple of months, and if it works out then we will move with you?" said Mama. Space was what she wanted. Mama needed space.

Baba went silent for a moment. Then he looked me straight in the eye. "Okay, Sara," he said. "You can stay here."

"Really?" I said.

Mama looked as surprised as I did.

"Yes. But I want you to know that if your mother and I divorce, it is your fault."

A clamour came from inside my parents' wardrobe. The door burst open and out ran Mama Cat. I looked at my mother, who was intent on the cupboard door, rather than on her husband. I got up and followed the cat out.

❦ ❦ ❦

IT IS HARD TO EXPLAIN sadness. It is not like pain. Pain is a cat's claws digging into your skin as you try to pat her to soothe the tears. Pain is surprise. A betrayal. There was some pain there for me. I knew that my father often got his words wrong, that he often said things without meaning them. But a large part of me felt like he meant it. It was easier to blame all of it—their problems, what seemed an inevitable solution—on me. No matter how much Nana tried to convince Mama how good the single life was, no matter how much Aisha drained their wallets, no matter how many fights Baba got in with Mohamed, it was my fault, all mine. They needed a reason, and I gave them one. I could play this part, even if it was painful. Sadness is different. Sadness is not sharp. It's heavy, the way it sits on your chest, filling your throat every time you try to breathe. Sadness is not understanding how to get up. But I could take the sadness, because right now, I could bear it more easily than they could.

❦ ❦ ❦

MAMA KNOCKED ON MY OPEN bedroom door. She sat at the end of my bed. "You need to change your sheets," she said. "When was the last time you changed them?"

"I don't know."

She dusted cat hair off my duvet.

"So," she said, "what's your decision?"

"What's yours?"

"It's our choice. If we choose not to go, it will just be... different."

I knew my mother needed me to do this for her. She would never do it on her own.

Baba always said that he and I had the same personality. That we follow our anger. That we are driven by what we think is right, and it leads us to rub people the wrong way. We see things in black and white. But I wasn't doing that here. I saw the grey. I saw that my parents were not evil or saintly. I saw that they were capable of harm and love at the same time, and worthy of care. I saw them as they were— two people half a world away from their true home, saddled with three kids and a recalcitrant mother. Two people who had no idea if they still loved each other, and perhaps did not, but were terrified to admit it. My parents were together because they were married in the eyes of God. All it would take was someone to call it quits. And right in front of us was an opportunity for me to make that call.

❧ ❧ ❧

BABA WENT TO CAIRNS ALONE, and Mama ordered a KFC bucket. Baba hated chicken on the bone. Mama said if there was one food she could eat for the rest of her life, it was chicken.

We ate until we felt sick. No one brought up anything about divorce.

We visited Baba in Cairns. Mama came too. It was a humid trip. We were only gone for a weekend, so we left Mama Cat in the house with a mound of food. She must have found comfort in our absence, because when we came back she had given birth—six little kittens licked clean of gunk, sitting at the bottom of my parents' wardrobe. Three of the babies didn't have tails. That was the Manx trait, from their father, Chaz. Baba's missing clothes had given Mama Cat enough room to make her own little safe haven.

❧ ❧ ❧

WHEN BABA CAME BACK AFTER two months, having not clicked with the people at his new job, all the kittens had found new homes. Early one morning, as I was leaving for school, I opened the front door and noticed a little tabby body lying in the middle of the road. I screamed. Our poor Mama had been hit by a car.

"At least she had her babies before she went," said Baba. "At least she has her legacy."

✿ ✿ ✿ RULE NO. 15 ✿ ✿ ✿

AVOID ABORTIONS

NANA ANNOUNCED TO THE SWEATY living room that she had had two abortions. The air-conditioning units were still sitting, uninstalled, under the stairs, where they had been since we moved in.

"You should do it, Soos," she said to me. "Do abortions. It's much more interesting."

"No," said Baba, by now settled uncomfortably back at home. It was a half-scream. "Haram. Do not."

They were talking about my Grade Eleven English assignment. We were to write a soapbox speech. My teacher, Ms. G, had told us to pick a topic we could talk about with passion. A controversial issue that we could really get into. Something sexy, she said. We didn't have to believe what we were saying, we just had to be persuasive.

"I've had plenty," Nana said. I wanted her to stop, but I also wanted to see how far she would go. "I can tell you all about them. It will be a good example for your speech."

I could see the veins in Baba's forehead about to breach the skin. He addressed her but was looking at me. "Stop," he said. "Enough. How dare you?"

In a blue-and-green classroom with posters on the walls reading *Bad grammar makes me (sic)* and *Shakespeare is everyone's cup of tea*, we worked on our speeches the next day. Carly tapped my desk softly with her fingers, as thin and white as paddle-pop sticks.

"Have you chosen yet?" she asked.

"I'm still tossing up between dole bludgers and abortion. You?" The choice between attacking welfare recipients or women's bodily autonomy was a hard one.

"Yeah, I'm still thinking too." Carly had topped the grade in English last year, and I knew she was going for a streak. She said she was thinking, but she had probably already shown a draft to Ms. G for notes and a pat on the back.

"Miss!" boomed a voice from the back. It was Jason. He was a six-foot-five egomaniac who referred to himself as "The Fridge" and coined his own catchphrase: "Say it to my neck." In Grade Nine he had held a kid up against a wall by the throat because the kid was wearing gloves in winter, and Jason determined that being cold made him a pussy.

"Hand up, Jason. Don't call out to me like I'm your servant," said Ms. G. "What is it you want?"

"Can I write my speech about how I hate Brett because he's a faggot?" He elbowed his friend Brett hard in the arm.

"Oi, fuck off!" said Brett.

Ms. G rolled her eyes.

Tom, on the other side of the room, called out, "Can you not? That word is fucking offensive."

"That's enough," said Ms. G.

I started typing.

Have you ever been raped?

I backspaced.

Have you ever had to carry the baby of your rapist?

Deleted.

Watch out, ladies. The government wants to control your privates.

Not it, either.

I thought about how mad Baba would be if he found out I was still talking about abortions at school. Even if I argued against them, the fact that I had entertained such a topic was enough to be a source of protracted disappointment.

Did you know that your hard-earned taxpayer dollars are going to waste on lazy old Bazza, who drives a Commodore and has never worked a day in his life?

"But wait, wasn't your family on welfare?" said Carly when I read it out. "You said you were on welfare when you came here, right?"

"Yeah, but it doesn't matter. Ms. G said we don't have to believe what we say."

"So you're happy saying something you don't believe?"

"Sure. It's just an assignment."

❧ ❧ ❧

THE NIGHT BEFORE WE WERE due to present, I practised my speech on Nana while I brushed her hair. It was matted at the back. It took effort to get out the knots. I sat on the back of the chair, my feet on the arms.

"You should have done abortions," said Nana. "No one cares about welfare."

"Some people do."

"Who? No one."

"Then why are they called *dole bludgers*? Obviously, someone cared about them enough to give them a name. And besides, I don't want to upset Baba."

"Am I considered a dole bludger? I get a pension."

"Maybe. But I don't really believe what I'm saying. I just have to say something."

"Okay, I see. Like propaganda." She sipped her hot tea. "You can't go through life not doing things out of fear of upsetting your father, you know. I will tell you now, you will upset him. Everything you do will upset him. You have to be prepared for that."

"Not if I do what he says. Not if I don't upset him on purpose."

"Even then. You will upset him."

Nana didn't take care of her hair the way she used to. She'd started having trouble lifting her arms. She couldn't reach the back. She said it was arthritis.

"Why did you say you've had abortions?" I said. "When you had miscarriages?"

"I would've had three girls, not just one. You would've had two aunties."

"Yes. But you said *abortions* when you were talking to Baba."

"Well. Maybe I did have abortions. None of his business, anyway. Men like him don't always know the difference."

"I think he does."

"Well. Then I upset him on purpose."

❧ ❧ ❧

ON PRESENTATION DAY, CARLY VOLUNTEERED to go second. I didn't know volunteering for second was something we

could do, but Ms. G accepted. Second was the best spot. Not
first, not breaking the ice, but early enough to get it over
with quickly.

Overconfidence in hand, Jason went first. His bigotry was
well publicised, mostly by Jason himself, so it was anyone's
guess what he had picked to talk about. I suspected he still
had his heart set on homophobia, but there was nothing stopping him going after anyone. I hoped I wouldn't be his target.

He started with a grunt to clear his throat.

"All gays," he said, "are pedos."

For the next ten minutes the class watched as he spat his
vitriol, all while Ms. G marked him on a criteria sheet. Half
the class were sunk in their chairs. Jason's mates were sniggering. And no one said a word until he was done.

"I have a question," said Tom. "Do you really believe all
that?"

Jason cleared his throat again but did not look at him.
"Yeah, man. Every word." He sat down in his seat next to
Brett.

Carly was getting ready for her turn—I could hear her
tapping her palm cards on her desk—but it was hard to take
my eyes off Tom. His face was red, and he was rubbing his
lips together. In his hands were his own palm cards. He was
ripping the corners off them bit by bit.

"Alrighty," said Ms. G. "Carly, you're up."

Carly stepped to the front of the room. I hoped to God she
hadn't picked homophobia too, but I knew it was unlikely.
As much as I thought she was a sellout, I knew she wasn't a
bad person. I couldn't help but feel a little pride in her. That
was my friend.

As Carly set up her PowerPoint, I started to sweat a little. Maybe dole bludgers was a bad idea. Maybe there was someone on welfare in the room. Maybe this was a set-up to make me look like a bad person. I didn't believe a word of what I was going to say in my speech, but I was going to say it anyway. I didn't want to be Jason.

She took a deep breath, and with her first words, came alive like a puppet on crack. She was a different person. She didn't look nervous at all. I could tell by the way she spoke that her speech was memorised. She didn't need the cards; they were just a prop.

"Australia," Carly said, "should not allow Muslims into the country."

She didn't look at me while she spoke. The class sat and listened to every word. Ms. G offered encouraging nods while she made scribbles on the criteria sheet. Once Carly was done, everyone clapped. She sat down and I smiled at her. I assumed she didn't mean it.

BABA

I FOLLOW MY FATHER INTO JIMMY'S. We come here sometimes when he's sick of Kofta Burger. Baba claims to have invented the kebab pizza that is now on the Jimmy's menu.

"I felt like pizza one day," he says, "but I also felt like a kebab. And I said, Jimmy, can you make me a pizza with kebab meat, and Jimmy looked at me like I was crazy. It had never been done before. Never. I made it. It is my invention. And now look." He points to the menu.

The shop is not called Jimmy's, but Baba calls it Jimmy's because that is what he calls the owner. I am doubtful that Jimmy is the owner's name, because every time Baba comes into the store and calls him Jimmy, there is a look of confusion on Jimmy's wife's face, who also works there. Perhaps Jimmy thought it would be too much effort to correct my father.

"Jimmy is so successful, all thanks to me," my father says.

We order two large pizzas. Baba has to have the kebab pizza every time. I order prawn with anchovy. He eats some of mine anyway. He explains the program he's on. It's called maintenance.

"They use something called Rituximab. They say it acts like a lock. You can imagine the cells like a pizza." He picks up a piece. A chunk of kebab meat falls off. I pick it up and eat it. "But there's a slice missing from the pizza. The slice is missing because the cancer affected this slice. And the chemotherapy I had killed this slice. It took it away. The Rituximab goes to the area of the missing slice and puts itself there to lock it. So, the cell will not grow in this space. Maintenance is all about locking the bad cells so they don't grow."

"So the bad stuff is gone?" I say.

"For now," he says. "I'm now on six months, every six months, locking in the missing piece."

I take a bite of the mixed meat. "I wish I could make good pizza like this at home," I say.

"One day you'll learn, habib," he says, "and you will have a husband and you will make pizza for him. And you will have a little baby and make pizza for the baby." He always finds a way to bring it up.

"Why can't I just make pizza for myself?" I say.

He pinches my cheek. "You can't eat pizza with me forever."

He complains of a stomach-ache. Jimmy comes out to our table to clear our plates and my father complains some more. Jimmy disappears into the back and returns with a cup of tea. "Drink this," he says. "It will make your stomach better." It is hot and milky.

Jimmy says his brother would make this tea all the time because he had stomach issues, and it would always help him. My father asks Jimmy if his brother still has stomach issues, if the issues are ongoing, because his are ongoing, and he doubts tea will help much—though he sips it as he says this. Jimmy says his brother died four years ago. I cover my mouth because a laugh is trying to escape. My father laughs. And Jimmy laughs. We all laugh together.

✿ ✿ ✿ RULE NO. 16 ✿ ✿ ✿

TRUST TOYOTA

I TRIED TO STAND STILL as the lady in the Department of Transport took my photo. She had big glasses that slid to the tip of her nose. She looked over them to see the computer monitor, defeating their purpose. The room was musty, full of people stuck to plastic chairs and holding paper tickets, waiting for their turn. I stood against a blank backdrop while the lady clicked around on the computer. I couldn't remember if I was allowed to smile or not. I decided to smile with my eyes. *Smize*, as Tyra Banks would say. I was still in my school uniform. I had my gold ribbon tied high on my head, and the wispy bits of hair that framed my face positioned just so. When I saw the photo, I was satisfied.

It was my sixteenth birthday, and I was going to learn to drive.

Baba said one's choice of car was a matter of life and death. He took me out for my first lesson in his Toyota Hilux, with its hard bench seats and narrow stick shift. Baba swore by Toyota. He said it was the safest brand there was, and he would never buy anything else.

I had never driven a manual before. He drove me to an empty carpark behind my old primary school. No one would be there on the weekend. He parked and pulled the hand-brake, but didn't get out of the front seat.

"I'm going to show you. Watch very carefully." He let the handbrake down. "Brake off," he said. Then he pushed the stick shift into reverse. His knees moved as he worked the pedals.

"What did you just do then?"

"Don't worry. That's reversing. We will get to that. Watch now. Are you watching?" He straightened the car up and pushed the stick shift forward. "First gear," he said.

"What does that mean?" I said.

"It's the first gear of the car." He moved his knees. "Clutch on while you do it."

"Is that the other pedal?"

"Yes. And then go." He repeated the same thing multiple times. Finally, he stopped and pulled the handbrake. "Yalla," he said, as he got out of the driver's seat. I shifted over into it. My legs weren't anywhere near the pedals. I felt for the lever to adjust the seat.

"Stop," he said, before jerking the seat forward for me. "Do the mirror—but make sure to put it back when you're done."

He got into the passenger side and fastened his seatbelt. "You don't have to learn this. Auto is more easier. There is no reason to drive manual here. Not like Egypt, where all cars are manual. Here, everyone drives auto."

"Then why do you drive manual?"

"Because I need to have this car."

I put the car into first gear.

"You need to press down harder on the clutch," he said. He was holding onto the door handle. "You need to push harder."

"I'm pushing hard," I said.

"Not hard enough. Do you hear that noise the car is making? Not hard enough."

We never left the parking lot that day, and Baba never took me for a lesson again. I tried not to take it personally, though part of me did. Learning to drive was a rite of passage, and he didn't want to undertake it with me.

When Mohamed learned to drive, my parents booked an Armenian-Egyptian-Australian guy to teach him. His name was Tov and they found him in the Yellow Pages. He looked a lot like my father. He had an accent that sounded like an Australian mocking a Lebanese accent—real thick, like he was speaking with a blob of yoghurt on his tongue at all times. He would answer the phone, "Hullo, this is Tov from Lively Learners," and he would do that even while he was instructing. He never wore shoes in a lesson and texted feverishly while his students tried to enter roundabouts. If they did the wrong thing, he'd stomp on his pedal control from the passenger seat, say 'watch it' and continue to text. It truly was Lively Learning. It was only natural that my parents employ Tov for me too.

When Mohamed learned to drive, he had his own car already. But I didn't. Every second Sunday Tov would pull up to the house a little late, in a blue Toyota Corolla. I ran out to the curb, where Tov was already standing, shoeless.

"How's the family?" he said, as he got into the passenger seat.

"They're good."

"How's Mohamed? Still on the road?"

"Yep."

"What's your Nan cooking today?" He was always interested.

"*Warak enab*." It was ten am and she had already started rolling the vine leaves.

"God. Warak enab. I haven't had warak enab in years. My wife doesn't cook. She's a bitch." He said often that his wife was a bitch. His wife was a white Australian. She was his second wife. His first had left him. He never told me that; I just made an educated guess.

I had a question to ask him, but I wasn't sure how to word it.

I didn't want him to say no, and I didn't want him to tell my father. "Do you teach manual?" I said, although I already knew the answer. I had seen a car with the Lively Learners logo stalling around the neighbourhood, with his other students in the driver's seat.

"Sure do. Do you want to have a go?"

"I've already tried once. On my dad's car. But I'd like to try again."

"Okay," he said. I thought it would take a little more to convince him. He wasn't as cautious as my father. "Just remind me next time so I bring the other car."

"Is it a Toyota?"

"No. It's a Hyundai."

"Oh."

"A Getz. Is that a problem?"

"I hope not."

❧ ❧ ❧

THE NIGHT BEFORE MY FIRST manual lesson, I had a dream that Mama left Baba for a white man. He had straight grey hair and no beard. He smoked cigarettes, but in a stylish way. He drank wine out of a fancy glass at a mahogany dining table. In the dream, I was sitting under the table, crying, while I saw my mother's legs beside those of this new man. I could never imagine Baba with a white lady. Not like I could imagine Tov with his wife. His wife, who was a bitch.

❧ ❧ ❧

TOV WAS A CHRISTIAN. A string of rosary beads with a cross hung from the mirror of the Getz.

"I have these here because I always say a little prayer before I take off in this thing," he said. "She's safe but, you know, some of these kids are crazy. They don't know how to drive. But I guess that's what I'm here for, hey?"

We were still sitting in front of the house. "I don't think I can go from here," I said.

"Why? Where else would you go from?"

"I've never driven a manual around other cars before."

"That's why I'm teaching you, isn't it?" He kicked off his shoes.

"I don't know if I can drive on the road."

"Where else are you going to drive? On the moon? Come on."

My hands were clammy as I tried to pull on my seatbelt.

"You gotta yank it hard," he said. "It gets stuck sometimes."

The smell of the car reminded me of old taxis in Egypt—most likely the melted rubber dashboard.

"What are you watching on TV these days?" he said, to help settle my nerves.

"Um. Not much. Mostly *America's Next Top Model*."

"Ah. No, I don't watch that. My wife, she loves that sort of stuff though. Kardashians. She loves that sort of stuff. She has a thing for Armenians!" He laughed.

"Nana watches them too."

"The Kardashians?"

"Yes, she's obsessed."

"Ah. Your Nan has good taste. Or maybe terrible taste. Can she make me some warak enab? I'm starving in that house of mine. All right. Let's go."

The sound of the car coming to life as I turned the key startled me.

"She's an old thing," he said. "That's normal. Don't worry about that."

❧ ❧ ❧

A COUPLE OF MONTHS LATER, Mama bought herself a new car. A red Hyundai Getz. It was sitting outside the house when I got home from school; she'd left work early just to pick it up. She let me practise in it. It was automatic, and small, so easy to manoeuvre. She said when I got my full licence, I could have it.

I gave up on learning manual. During my last lesson with Tov, he told me he didn't really hate his wife. "I just really hate her cooking. But she can learn, right?"

"Sure," I said. I felt a little guilty leaving Tov, but I knew he would be okay. And, I hoped, so would his wife.

The rest of my hours were spent with Mama, working towards getting that red Getz. Baba never got in that car. Not once. He thought my mother was trying to kill herself, and that she was taking me down with her.

MAMA

AN ANGRY, CURLY-HAIRED GIRL, backpack on, waiting at the
door. Nana says this is what my mother would do every day
after they ran away from Melbourne and returned to Egypt.
They lived above a travel agency, and my mother threatened,
daily, to buy a ticket.

"She would stand at the door and shout, 'I want to go
home. I hate it here. I want to go home.' And I would tell her
that we were home. But she didn't believe me."

My mother has never seen Egypt as her home, even
though she spent most of her life there. Now, when I ask
her about it, she says she would rather pull all her hair out
than go back. She says it's the bureaucracy. That nothing can
ever get done in that place. She says they do it on purpose.
Everything is slow for a reason. She's made her home here,
in Australia, where she's always wanted it to be. Of course,
each place comes with its own problems, but she would take
this country over that one any day.

It's unfortunate that she has started to hate our neighbours, in this place that she loves so much. The bougainvillea
petals from my mother's tree were getting in their pool.

If she had known, she said, she would have dealt with it. If this were Egypt, the neighbours would argue about the tree for years and nothing would get done about it. In Australia there is no talking—there is just cutting. She thinks the neighbour waited until she was at work to cut the tree. It was a strategic move, she says. It was his right to cut it, because the branches were creeping across the boundary. But he didn't just trim the branches, my mother says. There is a stump where the tree once was.

My mother does not shout often, but now she is shouting at our neighbour. I have never seen her this angry. "How dare you cut my tree," she says. "That is my tree, and you have no right."

The neighbour calls her crazy.

She says there is no way he was able to cut the tree that low from his side of the fence. She accuses him of coming onto her property and cutting her tree.

The neighbour says he will call the police if she doesn't leave him alone, and closes the door.

If he called the police, the police would come. Not like in Egypt, where no one would even think of calling the police over a tree. If they did think of it, and the police did come, they would expect a bribe.

Like Nana, I find it hard to understand why Mama loves Australia so much. The memories she's shared of her younger childhood here haven't always been pleasant.

"They called me wog at school," she said. "They put me in the wog class, with the Greeks and the Lebs. The teachers often made kids from the wog class wash the staffroom dishes. There was a redhead called Geraldine who came up to me in the playground and said I was just one big freckle. She said I smelled of fetta."

One day, while ten-year-old Mama was standing at the door, there was a knock on the other side. Nana tells me that Pa travelled from Melbourne all the way to Egypt to win her back. It sounds romantic, but it wasn't. He had come to Egypt to make sure she knew that he had refused the divorce. "I told him to divorce me," says Nana. "I already had a man I was interested in at the time. So I told him, 'Divorce me!' And your Mama's father said no. He said he will always be my husband."

In Egypt, things are different. You need both parties to agree that they've had enough of each other. Things are slow, even if they are inevitable. But in Australia, it only takes one side. Things get done.

❧ ❧ ❧ RULE NO. 17 ❧ ❧ ❧

WAIT FOR A RING

WHEN SHE WAS TWENTY-SIX, Mama's best friend got engaged to Baba's brother. That's how they met, she and Baba. She would go to his office in Alexandria sometimes and help him out with paperwork, she said. The brothers were managing their father's business at the time. After a few platonic visits, Baba called Nana and asked if he could marry her daughter. She said okay.

When I was eleven years old, I invited nine girls and one boy to the movies for my birthday. Baba answered the phone when the boy called to RSVP. Baba hung up the phone almost immediately and told me the boy would not be coming. No boys would ever be coming.

The thought of bringing a boy home to my family as a teen made me physically ill. But that didn't stop me from wanting to do so. I always wondered what it would be like to have a boyfriend. It might never be possible, but at least it was okay to wonder.

"There is no such thing as boyfriend–girlfriend," Baba would remind me every once in a while. "There is only husband and wife."

"But how do you ever get to know someone if you're never boyfriend–girlfriend?" I'd ask.

"You get engaged. That is how you get to know them."

My parents were engaged for nine months before they got married, but it didn't seem to have helped.

When I was sixteen and a half, Mama began to start work early, in order to finish at three pm. I was told it was so we didn't have to pay for after-school care for Aisha. Part of me also thought she wanted to keep an eye on me. She would pick Aisha up first, then me. Aisha always hogged the front seat. Every afternoon I could see her head bobbing up and down, complaining about something or other, as they approached my school gate.

The car rides were convenient, as I had started playing the trombone as well as the baritone. Lugging two heavy cases home would have been difficult. A group of boys, including Jason, would loiter around the gate after school, harassing people as they walked past. "What you got in those cases? Bombs?" he'd say to me, and laugh at his own joke. I would ignore him.

At sixteen, I had had a crush on about as many boys as I had years of age. When I say crush, I mean some form of attraction due to some form of interaction, often modest. I worried it would come to the point where if Jason were to ever say something to me that wasn't an overt racist insult, I would get a little tingle.

It seemed as though every girl at school had a boy-friend. Even Carly had one, who smelled of Vegemite scrolls. But I couldn't understand how I would go about getting a boyfriend, let alone keeping one. I had never had a boy express any interest in me. I didn't know what that looked like. I envied girls like Carly. Their parents who shared romantic stories about meeting and dating. They had blueprints to follow. I, on the other hand, was trying to assemble Apollo 11 with instructions that came from a NutriBullet.

There was a boy who sat at the end of the back row in band named Max. He played bass guitar, the incongruous electronic instrument in wind orchestra, and needed to be close to the power point. He really shouldn't have been in wind orchestra, given he did not play a wind instrument, but he was that good, Ms. H couldn't risk a bass section without him. I had never seen him speak to a girl before. I wouldn't call what he had a bowl cut, but it was bowl-cut adjacent. There was a mole on his face that looked like it could turn cancerous. And thick eyebrows—thicker than mine. He sat next to me in band when the trombonist was away. The cord of his base guitar had to stretch a little further, but he did it anyway.

I was the only girl in the back row. There was absolutely no competition.

In the week I decided I would make Max like me, he got the flu.

I found him in one of the rehearsal rooms of the music block, drool dripping down his bass guitar. I called his name from the door. He didn't hear me. I called again, and he sat up. This was the first time we had spoken.

"Sorry," he said. He seemed a little shivery.

"Ms. H said to pack up."

"Okay."

Egyptians say *el shatra tighzil birigl homaar*, which means a smart girl can knit even if all she has is a donkey's leg. With Max, I was about to make a sweater.

I told Carly I liked Max, and I told her to tell him so, and she did. She owed me after the racist soapbox speech. I put myself in his shoes: never had a girl's attention, and all of a sudden there was one right there, wanting to talk. Carly told me that when she told him he said, "Right." She was the second girl he had ever spoken to.

I didn't know what I was expecting him to do, but he did nothing. He was away from school the next day. I added him on MSN, but he didn't message me.

After days of his absence from school, I decided I had to make the first move.

Hi. So I heard Carly spoke to you.

Hi. Yeah.

I'm guessing you don't like me then. It was a disingenuous opener.

Well. I don't really know you.

Perhaps I was asking too much of the boy to declare his love for me straightaway. So I decided to ease him into realising he wanted to be my boyfriend. His MSN profile picture was a cartoon hooded figure that looked like something out of *RuneScape*, after all.

You're sick, aren't you. Or are you just avoiding me?

Yeah. I think I have a virus.

Gross.

As the repartee continued, he told me that he worked at KFC, and that to make the gravy they used the old fat at the bottom of the fryer.

My mum loves KFC, I said.

Nice.

I won't tell her about the gravy.

Probably for the best.

Do you think you would like me if you got to know me?

I think so.

❧ ❧ ❧

ONCE HE GOT OVER HIS virus, Max would wait for me at the front gate every day after school. We would stand there talking until we saw Mama's car approaching, and then he would leave before she had a chance to see him. Eventually, he began hanging out with me at lunchtime too. He wouldn't eat; he would just sit.

Once we were sitting together, my knee touching his. A teacher on duty came over and beckoned to me with his index finger. I felt ill, just as I had when Baba answered that boy's call. I had been found out.

"What's that?" said the teacher. He was wearing a piano-key necktie. He was a Maths teacher, but not mine.

"What's what, sir?" I said.

He pointed to my neck. Around it was the gold chain Baba had given me, the one with the word *Allah* on it.

"No jewellery at school. You should know the rules," said the teacher.

"But I thought we were allowed if they were religious symbols." One out of every three white girls at school had a cross around their neck.

"That doesn't look religious to me," he said.

"But it is."

"Take it off. Or I'm sending you to the office."

I unclipped the necklace and slid it into my skirt pocket. I walked back to Max, embarrassed. He didn't say anything. A boyfriend is meant to stand up for his girlfriend. But we weren't boyfriend–girlfriend, and I didn't expect him to understand. At least he didn't bring it up, so I didn't have to talk about it.

❧ ❧ ❧

ON DAYS WHEN WE HAD rehearsal, Max would carry my instruments for me from the music block to the front gate. I liked it. I knew what I was feeling wasn't necessarily love, but I sat in it anyway. It was nice to have someone there.

"Watch out!" Jason yelled to Max as we passed him on our way out. "She might have bombs in those cases." He didn't have much of a repertoire.

"You're hilarious," I said. Being around Max made me feel a little surer of myself.

After six months of carrying things for me, Max gave me a ring at lunchtime. It was a simple silver band with a small sapphire in the middle.

"Does this mean we're getting married?" I said, half joking.

"Maybe."

I wore it for the rest of the day. No teachers pulled me up for it. Maybe, I thought, this type of jewellery was acceptable.

In the afternoon Max walked me to the gate as usual. As we were waiting for Mama, Max said, "Your dad will never let us be together, right?"

In that moment, a spell was broken. Everything about Max became ugly to me. His bowl cut. His eyebrows. His mole. His cowardice. We hadn't even talked about the rules. He had done his research, exposing me before I had a chance to explain.

❧ ❧ ❧

I HAD FORGOTTEN TO TAKE the ring off before Mama picked me up. "Where did you get that from?" she said immediately. She seemed to see it even with me sitting in the back seat. I took it off and stuffed it into my pocket. My necklace was still in there. It must have gone through the wash.

"Carly gave it to me. She said I could borrow it."

Mama didn't say anything, but the look in her eyes in that rear-view mirror made me think she knew everything.

MAMA

THE ENGLISH GIRLS SCHOOL IN Alexandria is where my mother learned to pray. Nana never prayed, and her father only ever did so on Fridays. But there were devout girls at that boarding school, one from Nigeria, and one from Turkey, who taught her the proper way to do it. They taught her how to connect with her faith five times a day.

Nana tells me that my mother had a boyfriend at that school. A young man who went to the English Girls School, despite the fact that he was not a girl. He was not a boarder, and his name was Charlie. His parents were English, expats living in Alexandria, although he had the nose of an Arab. Nana says Mama and Charlie used to skateboard together. I wonder what it would be like to know my mother at that age. On wheels and free. I wonder if she wore a helmet.

Nana says Charlie asked my mother to marry him when they were seventeen. She wanted to, Nana says. She wanted to very badly. But she demurred. Her father would never let her marry an Englishman. A *kafir*. She never asked him, but she didn't have to. The next year Charlie moved back to England with his family.

Mama says that she was never with Charlie. They were friends. Yes, they would skateboard together. Yes, they went to school together. But the rest was a fiction. Nana made it up, Mama says. Nana embellished because she likes a story. I'm not sure I believe her.

I've seen a picture of Charlie on Facebook. He has been married, divorced and married again. He has kids, and his Arab nose still features. Last month my mother travelled to England without us, and she returned with a funny story. She had seen Charlie, who said that his mother had confessed a secret to him. His father was not the Englishman he had grown up with. His father was Syrian. An Arab, like us. Maybe Muslim. That explained the nose.

I wonder what my mother's life would have been like if she had known this earlier. Perhaps I wouldn't have been born. But maybe she would feel more alive.

DON'T STAY OUT LATE

THE CONFERENCE ROOM WAS DEEP in the school office, where students were never allowed to go. Not even teachers were allowed in there. Only school officials. The only reason Ms. G was present was because she had been promoted to deputy principal, and she was in charge of the elections. With me and Ms. G at the table were about ten other kids, all waiting to hear our fates.

Ms. G gave a spiel about how we all did a fantastic job with our speeches. How she could see us all as captains.

"It was a very close race. But the results are in. The four school captains of 2012 will be ... Gerard ..."

Gerard made a face that was half glee, half pain, like he had just been punched in the stomach. He had sweat patches under his arms. Like he had anything to worry about. Gerard was unimaginably popular, and impossible to hate. He had given his speech in a Morph suit. He was, in all senses, a goofball. I imagined his name was on every student's voting ticket.

"Dana..." Dana nodded, keeping a poker face. I knew if she didn't hear her name she would have exploded and murdered every person in that room, then burnt down the school. She was a type-A personality. An overachiever. She did cadets, and she was a little scary.

"Phillip..." The Samoan boy from my Maths class. He was reserved, but had an infectious laugh that made him easy to get along with.

"And... Sara." I realised I had been clenching my teeth, because when I stopped my jaw was on fire.

I had run for school captaincy for the same reason the other kids did—to feel important. To feel like I had some sort of control. To get validation. I wasn't entirely surprised I had won. There wasn't a lot of competition, and I had a solid strategy. My speech was full of jokes like *My leadership skills are as strong as the foundations of the pyramids of Giza and I'm not a terrorist, but I'm about to blow up this system. Vote for me for longer lunch breaks!* And the voters liked that. It wasn't that I thought they wouldn't like me because I was Muslim; they just liked me more because I made it known that it was okay to be overtly racist to me, if the mood were to ever strike them. I was their racism hall pass.

❦ ❦ ❦

THE END-OF-YEAR AWARDS night was tradition at Victoria Woods, and so was the initiation that followed. On stage, the past captains placed their blazers on us in a symbolic gesture of passing on the torch. Offstage, they told us to meet them at McDonald's after the event. We were to bring a candle and a lemon. We had to be initiated, earn our public blazer-drape in private.

Mama was in the audience. After the ceremony, she told me she was proud of me.

I wouldn't be home straightaway, I told her. Just a small celebration with my co-captains.

"Okay. But don't be out too late. Ten maximum." It was nine o'clock already.

I said goodbye to Mama, and rushed over to Gerard, Dana and Phil.

"Do you have your stuff?" said Dana.

"Yeah. I don't get what it's for, though."

"Apparently that's part of it. We're not meant to know."

"Where are they?" said Phil.

"Probably already at McDonald's."

I drove Gerard, and Phil went with Dana. Gerard pawed around my car, opening the glove box. He pulled out a CD: *The Lion King on Broadway.* "Is this all you have?"

"You can use the AUX," I said.

He pulled his phone out of his pocket and showed me the screen. It was smashed, and when he pressed the home button, the fractures lit up in a pixelated rainbow. "I cannot."

"How did you manage that?" I said.

He shrugged, and inserted the CD. "The Circle of Life" started. "A classic," he said. "This version sounds more cultural."

"What does that mean?"

"You know. Like, African."

I laughed. "Right."

He stuck his head out the window and started singing loudly. I told him to stop, tugging on his sleeve, but that only made him louder. Finally, when a new verse began, he pulled his head back in.

"Do you think we'll be good captains?" he asked me.

"I hope so."

"I'm afraid I'm going to fuck up somehow. Or, like, that people will expect things from me that I can't deliver."

"Me too," I said. "I think they picked me and Phil so we could be the *cultural* ones."

"What do you mean?"

"The brown ones."

"Isn't that a good thing, though?"

"I guess. I don't know. I just feel like they wouldn't have picked me otherwise."

"I don't think they would've picked me if I didn't come out in a Morph suit."

"You're right. But you get to shed that skin. I'm stuck with mine."

Gerard paused. "That was deep." He stuck his head out the window and belted out the chorus of "I Just Can't Wait to Be King."

❦ ❦ ❦

DANA WAS RIGHT. WHEN WE arrived at McDonald's, the four former captains were already at a table.

"No need to get yourselves anything," said the main one, Sean. "We've got this."

We sat down. Sean picked up the bun of the Quarter Pounder. Then he picked up the bubblegum McFlurry and poured it into the burger. He replaced the bun. "Eat it," he said.

"Who?" said Phil.

"One of you. Eat it."

"I'm not doing that," I said.

"I'll pass," said Dana.

"I'll do it," said Gerard. He picked up the burger. Ice cream dripped around his knuckles as he bit into it.

Once he was done, the former captains got up from the table. "Follow us," said Sean.

They entered the kids' play area, and climbed up the slide and into the compartment with a rocketship window. We climbed in after them. The slide was sticky from children's Fanta fingers. We all huddled in the small space. It was hot, and everyone was sweating.

"To be a good leader," said Sean, "you have to be vulnerable."

I wondered if this had anything to do with the lemon and the candle. I imagined them burning our naked skin and squeezing the juice into the wound.

"You have to tell us an embarrassing story about yourself."

I was disappointed. I was expecting torture. To earn my place. To prove myself. But this was soft.

"I think Phil should go first," said Dana.

"Why me?"

"Because I said so."

"All right, Phil," said Sean, "what's your story?"

Phil sat quietly, thinking for a moment. Then he spoke.

"So, it was Grade Five. Lunch break. We were in the middle of a game of tag. It was intense. Probably the best game we had ever had. I was caught up in it. So intense."

"What does an intense game of tag even look like?" said Gerard.

"Oi," said Sean, putting his finger to his lips. "Go on, Phil."

"Anyway," said Phil, "all of a sudden I felt a really really strong need to go to the toilet. I ignored it because I could not miss out on this game. So I kept playing. But then the turtle-necking began."

"Fucking yuck," said Dana.

"Shut up, shut up," said Sean. "Let the man finish."

"And as it happened," Phil said, "I did something stupid. I was trying to escape being tagged. I was at the top of the playground, and the only way out was the slide."

"No," I said.

"If you just imagine pressing a soft chocolate bar against the wall, that's what happened to my favourite red boxers."

"Dude," said Gerard.

"Anyway, after the incident I bolted to the bathroom and tried to clean myself. I even had a friend try to help me. Fast-forward to after-school care, where we were sitting out on the deck of the demountables, and the carer had a clear look of disgust on her face, her eyes scrunched up at the smell of something putrid. She looked at the bottom of her shoe to see if she had stepped in anything. I copied her and looked at my shoe too, knowing full well the issue was not my sole.

"I survived that, and as my mum picked me up and we walked away, I told her that I had kaga'd myself. That means poop in Samoan. What made it worse was that she wasn't angry at me. She just pitied me. Anyway. Moral of the story is: no game of tag is worth it. Just go when you gotta go."

The group was silent for a moment.

"Hey!" called a voice from the bottom of the McDonald's slide. "I'm going to ask you once to get out of there. If you don't, I'm calling security." This reprimand is what I had feared, but I was relieved it had finally come. Breaking the rules was not my forte.

One by one we slid down the slide.

"Sorry," I said to the manager, who looked younger than me.

She huffed, before locking the door to the play area.

The former captains led us towards the road.

"Where are we going?" I said.

"See that?" Sean pointed to an abandoned trolley in the park across the road. "One of you has to ride down the hill in that."

Gerard perked up. "I'll do it," he said, already running, not at all watching for traffic.

"No," said Dana. "I'm doing it." Gerard looked a little disappointed, but held the handle of the trolley while Dana stepped in. "Sitting or standing?" she asked.

"Hm. Now that you mention it. Standing," said Sean.

"I've got to go," I said. I didn't have to check my phone to know it was past ten. "My parents will be mad I stayed out this late."

"C'mon," said Dana. "At least watch me do this."

"I really have to go."

"Me too," sighed Phil.

"I'm not taking you home now, Phil. You have to watch me," said Dana. Gerard rocked the trolley back and forth as she spoke. She had great balance.

"I'll take you," I said to Phil.

"Pussies!" said Dana.

"Phil, you earned your place. But you . . ." Sean looked at me.

In the car we were silent. I figured Phil had had enough intimacy for the evening. I drove fast, speeding up the main road and past the school. Phil didn't speak. He seemed to share the urgency of my situation. As I dropped him off at his house, he said, "My parents are going to kill me for being out this late."

"Same."

He smiled. "White people never understand."

As soon as he closed the door, I sped off again. The roads were empty, striped in an orange glow from the street lights. A traffic light turned red. I was the only car at the intersection. Slowly, I snuck forward. Only a little bit. Front wheels over the white line. Then the back. The light went green before I could officially run the red. I was too pussy to break the rules, even with no one watching.

I pulled into the driveway and ran from the car. I fumbled with my keys and opened the door. Baba was usually in the front room with the TV on, especially when I was out. He could see the driveway from this vantage, so he knew when I was home. But the couch was empty. I hadn't checked my phone since the ceremony, because I dreaded what it might reveal. I pulled it out of my skirt pocket, expecting to see a million missed calls. But there wasn't a single one.

I walked into the hallway and heard muffled voices. My parents were in their room with the door locked, screaming at each other. They were yelling mainly in Arabic, but I caught the words *twenty years* and *I hate you.*

I went up to my room and dumped my bag on the floor. The candle and the lemon were still there, wedged into the pocket on the side. I took my lunchbox out of my bag and went down to the kitchen. My parents were still yelling. I thought about opening the door to let them know I was home, but decided against it. I emptied my lunchbox out into the bin, and grabbed a box of matches and a knife from the drawer.

Back in my room, door closed, I lit the candle. As I watched it burn, I wondered what the former captains were planning to use them for. Perhaps they were just a decoy. But maybe they were for me. Gerard, Phil and Dana had played their parts. All that was left was mine, and I ditched before I could do it. Sean had expected more from me. He didn't even know me, but his words made me feel like a failure.

The candle started to melt. Wax dripped down my palm and to my inner forearm. It looked as though it was tracing my vein. It was only hot for an instant. The knife sat next to me on the bed. I thought about it. Just for a few seconds. I thought about Tamara, how she never expected anything of me except friendship. I thought about what others had expected of me: Mama, Baba, Ms. C, Ms. H, the kids at school. Even Lilly. They all had their own idea of who I should be. I thought about how I hadn't heard from Tamara for so long. I thought about the lines on her legs I had seen at the beach. I thought about it. Then I couldn't. I blew the candle out. I picked up the lemon and bit into it. It was sour as hell.

BABA

BABA CALLS THE WAY HE lives his life trading with Allah. Do good things, and Allah will give good things in return. Like karma.

"But what if someone has a lot of bad things happen to them?" I say. "Does that mean they are a bad person?"

"Maybe," he says. "It could be that they are bad, or have done something bad, but not always. Sometimes bad things happen as a test of fate. Not as a trade for actions." He explains with a surah from the Qur'an.

"This surah, it's about a cow. It's talking about when the people asked Moses, 'If you have a god, get your god to send us a good meal. Get him to fill our table.' You know, asking Moses to prove that Allah exists. That's what this surah is about. Having faith, even if you can't see. Having faith in Allah, and the fate that he has designed for you." He pulls one of his copies of the Qur'an off his bookshelf. This one has English translations. He only uses it when I'm here.

"The main thing here is about believing in what happens without seeing a reason," he says. "For example, my sickness. A lot of people say, 'Why me, why me?' when they get sick.

No, it's not about 'why me.' Why you? Because Allah chose you to have this. He is testing you. Your reward for the test will come. The reward could be here or in the hereafter, but it will come."

"So if you do good things, good things will happen to you," I say.

"Yes."

"But if bad things happen to you, that doesn't mean you did bad things."

"No."

"It just means you will get good things later. If you survive."

"Yes. If you have faith in Allah, you will get good things later."

"So where does the cow come in?"

"It's not about the cow. You shouldn't need to see the cow as proof that Allah exists. *Iman*." Faith. "That's what it's about."

❧ ❧ ❧ RULE NO. 19 ❧ ❧ ❧

KEEP QUIET
AT THE TABLE

A YEAR HAD PASSED BY the time the four of us were sitting around a computer, Dana at the helm with the mouse, Phil, Gerard and I around her. We were editing our captaincy video, *The Year That Was*, a recap of all we had achieved together. There was a clip of Dana winning a national speech competition. Phil cooking for the homeless. All four of us at the swimming carnival, me wearing glasses shaped like marijuana leaves. Me a little teary-eyed in the next clip, after being told off by Ms. G for encouraging drug use.

Another clip showed our first school assembly as captains. Ms. G had told us that assembly was a formal occasion, and we should conduct ourselves appropriately, using formal language such as *good morning, students*, and *please rise for the national anthem*. The first thing Gerard said when he walked up to the podium was, "Wassup V-town? We got 'Advance Australia Fair' coming at you." I don't know if he just had a bad memory, or if he did these things on purpose to exasperate Ms. G. I envied him. These moments, as they

213

214 | MUDDY PEOPLE

flashed across the screen, had been my lifeblood. They were a distraction from my parents. I had spent large portions of the year worrying only about getting Gerard to pull his head inside the vehicle every time we neared a tunnel. Getting home on time didn't seem so important anymore.

Our last responsibility as captains was to interview the new recruits alongside Ms. G. We split into pairs. Dana and Phil interviewed one group, while Gerard and I took the other.

Our first interviewee was a tall boy named Aaron. I recognised him as a friend of Dana's. He had a kind but nervous smile, and the freckles on his cheeks bunched up as he squinted whenever he answered a question. I asked him what he would do for the school if he were successful in gaining school captaincy.

"More English tutoring support for students," he said.

"Are you a fan of English?" I asked.

"No. I hate it. I suck at it. That's why we need more tutoring."

"I have a question," said Gerard. "And this is an important one. Perhaps more important than any question you'll be asked in your life."

"All right."

Gerard cleared his throat. "Xbox or PlayStation?"

Ms. G laughed at Gerard's question in a way that I knew meant *if you weren't graduating soon, I would kill you.*

❧ ❧ ❧

BY THE END OF 2012, I had finished school, and my parents were divorced. I wasn't there when it happened. I've found out the details over the years since, by sitting at their dinner tables, hearing their stories as I jump between their homes. Why they stopped speaking to each other. Why they couldn't be amicable. How different their versions of the marriage were. My father thought my mother was playing a game. That's how he describes it. But because they were in different places, it was difficult to decide which rules to play by.

"I asked her," my father said, "very clearly. I said, 'You have two options. Do you want the law, or do you want the Sharia?'"

Sharia is the Arabic word for law. Sharia is the law as set out in the Qur'an. "And she wanted to take the best of each."

Under Australian law, assets are pooled and then split. Under Sharia, it's different: everyone keeps their own. Mama agreed to buy Baba out of the Victoria Woods house. The house she always hated. She decided to keep it. This wasn't expected, but it's what she wanted. The house was Australian law.

Then there were the overseas assets. The enigmatic assets. Inheritance, perhaps, or inheritance to come. There were things I didn't know about, and I knew she would never talk about. She wanted those dealt with the Sharia way, meaning they were all hers.

My father thought it was unfair that my mother picked and chose in this way. He believed that the settlement should follow one law and one law only. Either Australian or Sharia. But to my mother, it wasn't that simple.

They worked their way through their assets, deciding whether to split them or keep them on a case-by-case basis. My father went along with it. "I agreed to do it this way not because I thought it was right, but because I didn't want your mother to be able to use anything as an excuse against me," he said. "I went along with what she wanted because I didn't want a bad word said about me later. I played it all by her rules so she wouldn't have a word to say."

They left till last the biggest negotiation: their future. In Australia, only one petitioner is needed to initiate a divorce. But in Egypt, you are married under Sharia until both parties give their consent to dissolve the marriage. Mama wanted his signature. Even though my mother never intended to travel to Egypt again, she didn't want to still be married to my father in the eyes of the law there. She wanted to be severed from him, everywhere and entirely.

When my mother told me what my father asked her over that table with the lawyers, I didn't believe her. I knew Baba had his faults, but he wasn't a blackmailer. "He told me he would only sign the Egyptian divorce paper if I gave him money," Mama said. "A lot of money. Thousands of dollars. 'Either you give me money or I won't let you go.'"

When I brought this up to my father, he didn't deny it. But his version was different. "There are two ways to get divorced in Sharia," he said. "The first way, the man will divorce the lady. He has the right. He has the upper hand. He will divorce the lady because he does not want to be her husband anymore, for whatever reason, and that's it. He will give her her rights, of course, but that's it. But if the woman wants to divorce, this is different. If the woman is forcing a man into a divorce that he does not want, that's something else. They call it *khula*."

Khula. Removing a part. Taking a piece of a whole.

"Your mother wanted to take herself out—*akhlaa*, it is called," he said. "I didn't want any of this. It was her choice."

There's a hadith in the Qur'an about a woman named Jamilah. She was unhappy in her marriage. She went to the Prophet Muhammad and told him that she wanted to leave her husband. The Prophet said okay, but give him back your *mahr*—the dowry he gave when you got married. Give it back, then you can get divorced. This is what Baba said he wanted. "I paid your mother gold and bracelets and money. In the religion, she has to pay them back if she wants to apply for divorce in Sharia. She will tell you, *oh, he's asking for money for divorce*, but this is part of the Sharia. She's forcing the end of the relationship. That was her desire to destroy the family, not mine. So, to get out, she has to pay me everything back. I didn't ask for anything other than what was rightfully mine for return."

My mother interpreted the hadith differently. "In Sharia, you only give back the dowry if the marriage hasn't been ..."—she hesitated—"... consummated. So I think after twenty years and three children, I don't have to give back a bracelet. But I did. I paid him that money just to get that signature. Just to get myself away from him."

My father was not ashamed because he felt he did everything by the book. His book. "You mother had the intention to divorce me ever since she went to Hervey Bay. She said that to me. She said she'd stayed with me all those years because she needed me financially. When she realised she could be on her own, then that was it, she was prepared to get rid of me. So easy." I could see him getting upset. "You know what she said to me? When I was sitting there at that table with all her lawyers during the settlement? She pointed at me and she shouted, '*Issra kamaan ya harami! Issra kamaan!*

Steal more, you thief.' And I said, 'More? What have I ever stolen from you?' And she kept shouting, 'Issra kamaan!'"

My mother says, "If there is one thing in life I have learned, something I will never lose faith in, it's this: if it weren't for money, marriage wouldn't exist. If women had money, there would be no need for husbands. They would be on their own. And they would be happy. And that is a fact."

BABA

IT IS HARD TO PROCESS the idea of a family member dying. To contemplate the tragedy, even if it's just a possibility. It's three am and I am awake, in bed, at home. Mama told me not to come to the hospital until she gives the word. That's what she said when she left, almost five hours ago. She's not answering her phone, and I don't know what to do. So I continue to wait.

I am not good in these situations. Where there's a possibility of death. When we were kids, Aisha and I were jumping between our two beds when she slipped. She hit her head against the metal frame. It bounced off, her neck like a noodle. There was blood on the frame and spattered on the carpet. I thought she was dead, until she lifted her head. A massive gash ran across her forehead, dripping red. She didn't scream until I started. Nana put a Band-Aid on her, and she sat watching TV in a blanket for the rest of the afternoon. I asked her if she needed anything. She said, 'Can you make me some lunch?' Superstitiously, I thought that if I did, it would be her last supper, so I didn't. I ignored her request, and she turned out fine.

When we were packing up our house in Egypt, a rolled-up carpet was leaned against a table, with a glass-faced clock sitting on the floor beneath. Mohamed was running up the carpet, then jumping off the table, thumping onto the thin floors. I was watching, partly in admiration and partly in fear, thinking he might put a hole in the floorboards. He went up and down and up and down, and eventually he slipped. He fell off the table and onto his back, onto the clock. It shattered under his fat little body. Blood was everywhere. My parents ran over, screaming, scooped him up and took him to the hospital. It all happened so fast; I didn't get a chance to ask if I could come. Mohamed still has a thick, banana-shaped scar on his back.

❧ ❧ ❧

JUST BECAUSE BABA IS NO longer in the house doesn't mean he doesn't make his presence known. He calls at least once a day to check if I am breathing. I don't often ring him. I don't need to, because he beats me to it. So, when I do, he answers in a panic, because he knows something is wrong.

I call him at seven am after the long night. It is early February. The mosquitoes are already out, flying into the house because Nana has left the flyscreen open. She thinks it brings in more air this way. I have been scripting the conversation in my head all night.

I can hear the alarm in his voice as soon as he picks up. "Kheer?" he says. "What's happening?"

I immediately forget what I practised, and my voice goes wobbly. "Aisha is fine," I say.

"What?" His voice cracks. "What happened?"

"I'm trying to tell you. She is fine, but last night she was driving home—"

"Where is she?" he shouted. As though I am keeping him from her. "I need to see her."

"—and a wallaby jumped in front of her car. She's back from the hospital. She's asleep. I'll FaceTime you when she wakes up."

"No. I'm leaving. I'm coming now."

"You don't need to come. She is fine. But the car has been written off."

"What happened?"

"It rolled."

Baba says something quickly in Arabic that I do not understand, but I know he's asking Allah for something. I never considered my little sister dying before me. I'm glad she hasn't. In the last six months, two people have died in accidents on the same road.

When Aisha wakes up, she looks like shit. The cut on her leg is deeper in daylight. She got it when she crawled out the broken driver's side window. It's burgundy and blue, and runs half the length of her thigh. She's covered in mosquito bites—she says she could feel the mosquitoes as she waited for the ambulance. She hears a buzzing in her ear, but other than that, she is fine.

The car had landed on its roof. In the roll, it took down a nearby electrical pole. It's a miracle that she's alive. She never wants to drive again. Baba says it is lucky she was in a Toyota. In any other car, she would be dead.

A few days later, Aisha says she's still having ear trouble. She can't hear out of her right side. Sometimes, I forget and talk to her while standing to her right, and she struggles, not wanting to admit it.

Mohamed deals with stress differently. He doesn't talk to Aisha for two weeks. He doesn't ask her about what happened or if she is okay. He just acts like nothing happened. In a way, I can understand where he is coming from. Sometimes if you pretend, you can get on as normal. Baba says Mohamed acts this way because he's been the only man in the house for too long. He doesn't have a role model. The man is meant to protect his family, Baba says. To protect them from any harm that might come their way.

RULE NO. 20

NO SHOES IN
THE HOUSE

MY I HEART BJ T-SHIRT was my favourite souvenir from China. It was everyone in our group's pet purchase. Ms. H said that if she saw anyone buying them, they would have a week's detention when we got back to Australia. But that did not stop us.

Over time it had become worn. The red of the heart had turned pinkish. It had become my gym shirt.

I had joined the gym optimistically when it was offered as an alternative to organised sport at school. The owners were savvy: what to the undiscerning eye was a bunch of rowdy kids in on a Wednesday afternoon was to someone else a captive market of teens with budding body dysmorphia. After I graduated, I kept up the membership.

I avoided going on the floor on Wednesdays. It was hard to compete with boys hopped up on steroids. The only body I felt comfortable looking at was Aaron's—the boy I had interviewed for captaincy—because it wasn't covered in uncomfortably large and bulging veins. He wore long sleeves under a t-shirt when he worked out.

I used the group fitness room. It was an oasis of sorts. A room full of old white women and pop music.

"Okay, ladies," the trainer announced through her headset microphone, with a certain pep in her voice that sounded terminal, "are we ready to Sh'Bam?" She hit play. "Eye of the Tiger" pumped through the sound system. The women formed lines facing the front and started bopping from side to side, mirroring the trainer. I stood in the middle row. I wasn't confident enough to be in the front, but also felt those in the back could benefit from my superior sense of rhythm. I bopped with them as we made our way through the various tracks, each with their own dance style. Some involved a lot of jumping around.

"Yeah! Rock it out!" shouted the trainer at the room of seniors playing air guitar.

Next was a remix of an R. Kelly song. This was "the hip-hop track."

"Bounce the basketball," said the trainer. The ladies mirrored her movement of bouncing an invisible ball with two hands to the side of her body. "And throw the basketball." She moved her hands above her head, sweeping to the other side of her body, in a repeated motion in time with the beat. In Sh'Bam, hip-hop and basketball were the same thing.

We went through a couple of jazz and musical theatre tracks. The steps weren't difficult, but the repetition made me sweat. I'd watch the trainer pull it off with ease while speaking into the microphone, not passing a single heavy breath. You could tell she was a trained dancer. I wondered if she felt like a failure for having to teach us. She probably went home at night and cried into her fluoro tank top.

We eventually reached the cool-down track. The trainer took us through each stretch, making it obvious how much more flexible than us she was. I caught my breath as I hung down, trying to touch my toes.

I got home and kicked my shoes off outside the front door. I threw my sweaty t-shirt in the wash basket.

"Can you do your own washing from now on?" said Aisha.

"I never asked you to do my washing," I said.

"But you leave it for so long, and then I have to do it."

"No, you don't."

"Yep, I do."

Mohamed wanted to take us out for lunch. This was out of character, as Mohamed never offered to do anything, let alone spend money on us. Baba was invited, along with me and Aisha.

Baba had gotten a job in Katherine. When he visited, he did not stay in the house. So Mohamed suggested we meet him at Café Arabica.

Aisha and I arrived in my car. I offered to pick Baba up, but he refused, still holding a grudge against the Getz. He got a rental, and we waited for Mohamed to show.

A little while later, Mohamed's car pulled into the parking lot. We didn't need to see it because we could hear it. He didn't take care of the engine. When he walked in, he wasn't alone. He introduced the girl with him as Emma. She had brownish-reddish hair, the same shade as Carly's. Probably from the same box. She wore thick eyeliner. She was white and her hair was dead straight. She was pretty. This was his girlfriend.

I watched Baba speak to her, his smile never leaving his face. Asking her questions, like he was so interested in her life. He laughed pre-emptively whenever she said something, to make her feel funny, even if he didn't fully understand what she was saying. He even paid for her lunch. *Since when*, I thought, *was this okay?*

"Did you know about this?" I asked Baba in the carpark, once Emma and Mohamed had left.

"Yes," he said. "I asked for it."

"What?"

"I asked to see her. Aisha told me she thought Mohamed was talking to a girl. So I asked him and he said yes."

"But—"

"Boys can marry non-Muslim girls," Baba reminded me.

"I know. But they're not getting married. They're boy-friend and girlfriend. You said no boyfriend–girlfriend."

"Boys are different from girls," he said. "It's important to meet her. It's important to bring these things to the light, not leave them in the dark."

❧ ❧ ❧

WHEN EMMA CAME OVER TO the house for the first time, to meet Mama, she was wearing a tank top and sneakers, as though she and Mohamed had just been to the gym. She wore the sneakers in the house.

She ended up having a shower at our place, because she and Mohamed were going out for dinner. Her clothes went into the wash with my things. Once they dried, I hid them in my cupboard. I did this every time I found something of hers in the wash. Slowly she would have nothing left to wear, I figured, or if she was smart, she would realise she was not wanted and stop coming around.

It wasn't Emma herself I resented. I was happy that Mohamed had someone who would put up with his annoying habits, like chewing with his mouth open and breathing too loudly. I was bothered by what she represented—change for him, but not for me. She was an outsider. She was white. And she was acceptable. I had had dreams of bringing a white boy home to my father, and in those dreams my father disowned me. But for Mohamed it was so easy, and he didn't even see it. His privilege was invisible to him. And all I had were stolen clothes.

MAMA

THERE IS A PILE OF hard drives on the living-room couch. They're copies of all the files her father had on his computer, my mother says. She is sifting through them, connecting them to her laptop one by one, trying to find an inheritance I'm not sure even exists. She has found copies of certificates from banks confirming transfers and receipts, but they are all typed in Comic Sans and have grammatical errors peppered throughout, presumably written by the fraudsters who convinced my grandfather to hand over his money. I believe that whatever he had to leave was all scammed from him, but my mother doesn't think so. She has spent three days on her computer, trying to convince herself that he must have left her something.

Her bedroom floor is strewn with papers, a lot of them bruised with stamps. On her bed is an open passport and two death certificates, one in Arabic, another in English. The one in English says my grandfather died of a tumour in his colon. My mother said he had a lot of other tumours too, so it's a technicality that this was the one that killed him. The passport has a picture of him. It's the first time I have seen him in old age. The only images I have seen are from his wedding to Nana, when he was twenty-five, and the small one in my mother's wallet. His grey hair is a reminder that we lost a lot of time. The passport expires in four years. It is strange to think that we can expire before our documents.

She never speaks of the circumstances that led to her becoming estranged from her father, but Nana talks about it, of course. She likes to talk about it.

"The last time she saw her father was in a courtroom," says Nana. "She was twenty-one years old." It was about a house. All of this was about a house.

"Your mother was living with her father in a unit that was owned by his father—her grandfather. She wasn't living there by choice, mind you. No. Her father forced her to stay with him. He said, and I swear he said this, that if she ever spoke to me again, he would kill her. She was terrified of him. Absolutely terrified. Imagine, stopping your daughter from seeing her own mother."

"So you never saw her? At all?"

"I didn't say that. I saw her almost every day. She'd tell her father she was going to university, and she would come and see me. I don't know how she managed to pass all her exams, I really don't. She never went to university. Your mother is very clever."

"So her father and grandfather were basically keeping her captive."

"No! Her grandfather was a lovely man, really kind. He was hardly ever in that house. He would travel a lot. It was his son who was awful. When your mother was twenty-one, her father tried to claim the house as his own. He outright said it was his. He was trying to steal from his own father. He took his own father to court. If that wasn't bad enough, he asked your mother to testify. To lie to the judge and say the house belonged to him when it didn't. She knew it didn't. Can you imagine, telling your daughter to do that?"

There is nothing worse than puncturing your father's pride, no matter how wrong he is. My mother had the option to say nothing. She had the option to let it go. But she chose to do something, and it seems that decision has haunted her for thirty years. What she chose to do was write a letter and have it submitted to the court. A testimony. In that letter, she wrote that she lived in the unit with her father. That she spent every day in that house with her father. But the house did not belong to her father. That roof, and everything under it, belonged to her grandfather.

When her father read the letter, he gave up his ownership claim. His father kept the house and my mother was disowned. She moved in with Nana and never saw her father again.

There is an Egyptian saying: *You can pluck a chicken, feather by feather, and it will shriek in pain. But as long as you give it crumbs, it will follow you forever.* My mother thinks she knows her father so well; she is resolute in the fact he is hiding something. She is convinced there is more to find on these hard drives, that all he wants her to do is look a little harder. It's a game he's set up for her. She says she knows how his mind worked. This is what he would have wanted her to do. This is how he thought. She just has to follow the trail.

I imagine his ghost peering through the window at one am as she sits at her glowing laptop, glee in his eyes. If this reward exists, it is buried as deep as her father's bones.

❦ ❦ ❦ RULE NO. 21 ❦ ❦ ❦

NEVER TALK TO STRANGERS

THERE WAS A KNOCK ON the flyscreen and a call. "Hello?"

Mama and Nana were watching TV, and they didn't hear it. I looked down the dark hall to a large silhouette outside. I couldn't see who it was. It was about seven pm and we were not expecting anyone. Mohamed wasn't home, and the voice didn't sound like his.

"Hello?" I said back, loud enough for Mama to hear. "Who's there?"

The man shuffled back and forth. "I'm in a spot of bother," the deep voice echoed down our hallway. I didn't know what to expect, so I grabbed a knife from the woodblock in the kitchen. I held it behind my back and approached the door. I didn't know if I had the guts to use it. Mama came into the hallway and looked at me like I was insane. But the man's silhouette was huge, and he was being cryptic. The flyscreen was closed but unlocked.

"Can I come in?" he said. He had the voice of a man but spoke the words of a child.

"No," said Mama. She reached the door, flicked the lock and switched on the light. It showed a balding man wearing a striped khaki shirt. His thongs slapped the cement as he shifted back and forth. He looked in his late thirties.

"What do you need?" she said.

He repeated, "I am in a spot of bother."

His name was Justin, he said, and he was lost. Mama asked if there was someone who could come and pick him up.

"Yes," he said. "My dad. I live with my dad. I tried to call him, but he's not answering his phone." He pulled a phone out of his pocket. It was not a mobile. It was a wireless landline, taken off the hook and out of the house. It was then that I understood Justin was different from us.

"Do you know your dad's number?" said Mama.

"Yes," he said, and he recited it. She called it and there was no answer. She called it again and left a voicemail. Justin was pacing, scratching at his skin incessantly. The mosquitoes.

"Go get some spray," Mama told me. I felt a little worried about leaving my mother alone with a stranger, but I trusted her judgement enough. I went to the kitchen. I kept the knife with me and picked up a can of Aerogard.

When I returned, Mama was outside with Justin. She was waiting on the phone again, and she had brought a garden chair over for him to sit on. I went to hand him the Aerogard.

"Thank you," he said. He didn't take the bottle. Instead, he stuck out his arms in front of me. He wanted me to spray them. I did, and his legs too.

He asked me if we'd had tea. I knew he meant dinner. I said yes, and he looked disappointed.

"Have you?" I said.

"No."

After trying to get through to his dad for half an hour, Mama admitted that maybe the best option was to call the police. They could pick him up and take him home.

"No," said Justin, getting up out of his seat. "No. Please don't." Mama and I instinctively took a step back. "Can't you just take me home? To my dad's house. I know the address."

"I don't think that's a good idea," said Mama.

Justin looked like he was about to cry. "Am I in trouble?" he asked. This made me think he had been in trouble before.

"No. Of course not," she said.

❧ ❧ ❧

WHEN THE POLICE OFFICER ANSWERED the call, my mother explained the situation.

"Ah, yes." I could hear the officer's voice, even with the phone pressed to my mother's ear. "This isn't the first time Justin has been lost. I'll try and get in touch with his father. Can I call you back on this number?"

"Yes," said Mama, and she hung up.

I was proud of my mother. She was kinder than she needed to be to people. I could see she felt for Justin. Meanwhile, I still had a knife in my pocket.

A few minutes later, the phone rang again.

"It's your father," Mama said to Justin. She hadn't said that word in a while. Faaatha.

Justin lurched forward. "Can I speak to him? Please. Please."

Mama handed him her mobile. "Hi, Dad," he said. "Are you coming to get me?" Justin listened for a while. I couldn't hear what his father was saying, but he spoke for a long time.

"Are you still going to visit me tomorrow?" he said. The word 'visit' made me realise he was lying when he said he lived with this father. He handed the phone back to Mama.

Justin's father explained to Mama that Toby would come and get Justin. Toby was his son's carer. Mama hung up. "Why didn't you tell us about Toby?" she said. Justin shrugged.

The phone rang again.

"Yeah." I could hear Toby's voice. "Where is he?" Mama gave him the address, and Toby huffed. "I'm making dinner right now, you know. I have other clients, you know." He hung up.

We waited, mosquitoes buzzing around the light. "Is Toby a good cook?" said Mama.

"No," said Justin.

Hours later, once Toby had left and we were back inside watching TV, Mohamed got home. He was not gentle with the flyscreen. It clanged as he swung it open with too much force. Mama said he didn't know his strength.

"Where have you been?" I said. "We almost had a home invasion."

"No, we didn't," said Mama. "We were perfectly fine on our own."

❦ ❦ ❦ RULE NO. 22 ❦ ❦ ❦

TAKE OUT LIFE INSURANCE

I THINK ABOUT MY PARENTS dying, probably more often than I should. I don't want them gone. But I have moments of remembering that they are human, and so am I, and one day this will all fade to black. My father doesn't believe that. Neither does my mother. To them, there's got to be something else out there, a hereafter.

My mother has life insurance. I know because I heard my parents argue about it when they were together. My father is against the idea completely. He says he will never get it, despite being sick. He says it's haram to bet on your own death. He has given me an envelope with money to cover the cost of his funeral. He will leave his inheritance, of course. That gets split between the three of us, Mohamed getting half and Aisha and I a quarter each. That's Sharia. The brother is meant to take care of his sisters.

My father has been talking about his death for twenty years.

He has been dying for twenty years.

If there's one thing my father wants to see before he dies, it's his daughters married. For them to be off his hands. For a husband to come and take the lead. Of course, it can't be any man. There are requirements. He has to have money, enough to take care of us. He has to have a house. He has to be smart, but not too clever. He has to be firm, but not too hard. He has to be squeaky clean, but not afraid to roll up his sleeves. He has to, he has to, he has to. But, if he doesn't have all that, at the very least he has to be Muslim.

He invites men to the house. Old friends, from years ago, from Cairns and elsewhere. Friends who helped him out when he was alone. I tell Aisha that this is his way of introducing me to Muslim men, because I refuse to go to mosque with him anymore. This is his way of managing my future. Aisha doesn't believe me. She thinks I think too highly of myself.

One night, we cook prawns on the barbecue and we set the table inside. There are two men invited to dinner—Baba must be hedging his bets. I set five plates, but Baba says to set six. Mohamed is coming, he thinks. The brother is meant to be here for these sorts of things. I tell him that Mohamed is not coming. He is busy, at the gym or with Emma. Or he has forgotten. Baba tells me to set six anyway, just in case his son happens to come through.

I sit and I watch these two men eat. One is tall, with a head of curly hair and a scruffy beard. His name is Mohamed. He is wearing a white singlet because of the heat. Baba turns the air conditioning on, and I know the smell of prawns will be in it for days. The other man is shorter, but still taller than me. He has a lisp and blue eyes. He is also Mohamed.

A month goes by before I hear about the men again. Baba calls to tell me there's a boy who wants to be my friend. I know he is not a boy, he is a man. Both Mohameds were at least ten years older than me. Just friends, Baba says. What's wrong with friends?

"I really don't like this," I say. I can feel myself crying. Not because I am sad, but because I am scared of disappointing him. I try to always do as he asks. I know I need to gain credits with him. But I can't do this. "I really hate it when you do this."

"Do what?"

"You want me to be *friends* with people."

"Why are you crying?" he says.

"Because. I can't just flick a switch. No boys, then all of a sudden married."

"Who said married? I said just friends."

"I know what you're asking me, Baba."

"I'm just asking you to be friends. That's all."

"I'm not going to marry these people. I don't want to get to know them. People marry people they already know. That's how it works here."

"Well, we are not from here."

"Well, I am here. And you are here. And most of my friends are here."

"How will you get married if you never give it a chance?"

"I want to marry someone I like. Someone I can be real friends with first. I don't want to give chances to people I don't know."

"I'm not forcing you to do anything. I never forced you."

"I know you're not forcing me. But I think we're going to have to accept that I'm not going to marry a random brown person.

You have all these rules for me. All these standards. But the only rule that matters when it comes to my husband is that he is Muslim. The standard is so low. That's not fair."

"He's not random. I know—"

"You don't know if he'll be nice to me. You don't know if we care about the same things. And that's the basics. That's the minimum. I don't want someone just because they are there. I want someone I will care about." I can't bring myself to say someone I am *in love* with. "Just because someone is a Muslim doesn't mean they are a good person. He is a stranger." I take a breath and it hurts. "Chances are, and the chances are very big chances, I am going to marry someone who is white."

He is silent for a moment. "You know the rules," he says finally.

"Yes, I know."

"You need someone who knows the culture."

"I know."

"Someone who accepts the culture." I know he means a convert.

"But you're going to have to accept that they're not going to be Egyptian. Or Arab. Or anything like that."

"It sounds like you have someone in mind."

I don't say anything. My father wants me off his hands, but he doesn't want to lose me. "You don't have to cry, habib."

BABA

IT'S FUNNY HOW WE CENTRE ourselves in our memories. We are the heroes and the victims, even when the story isn't about us. My memories of my father's illness are focused on that hospital in the Gold Coast, the two of us together travelling to and from it for his treatment. I was there for it all, in my memories. Not my sister, who worked weekends. Not my brother, who rarely picked up his phone. I was the one who helped my father through the toughest time in his life. That's the story in my head. But there was a period that ran its course without me there: my father's time in Katherine. I don't think about it because I can't imagine it. I don't ask because I don't want to complicate my own narrative, my memories of me being a good daughter when my father was at his weakest. But the truth is, in the hardest parts, he was alone. He has to fill these blanks in for me.

He tells me, "When I was in Katherine, I was trying to lose weight. And I did. I dropped from 144 to 109 in about two months. I remember thinking how good I was, to do that. The lady at the gym reception said she didn't recognise me. And I tried to take this as a good thing. But her face said different.

Her face said something is wrong. She saw something in me, and it wasn't healthy.

"When I started to feel pain in my back, behind my kidneys, I went to my GP and he said it could just be normal muscular things. Everybody gets them. So I left it. I left it until it got really bad. Too bad.

"I decide to see another doctor, who is very nice to me. She is Egyptian too. It is funny that I am on the other side of the world, in a place so far away like Katherine, and I find another Egyptian. It is nice. She really seems like she cares about me. She says, 'We better put you in for CT scans.' I went for a CT scan in Darwin, because they don't have the machines in Katherine. When I got back to Katherine, I got a phone call from the GP. The results were back, and she mentioned a term I didn't understand. She was talking about enlarged lymph nodes. And I said, 'What does it mean?' She said, 'It's something we need to investigate.' And I said, 'But I don't understand: what is enlarged lymph nodes?' And she said, 'It means cancer.'

"'It's a blood cancer. Not an organ. Not something you can cut out. It's all over. In your blood.'

"I go to the oncologist to see what we're going to do. We do a biopsy. I was working full-time in Katherine. Back and forth, back and forth between Katherine and Darwin, 350 kilometres during the wet season, because in Katherine, they didn't have a facility for cancer treatment or anything. They have a general emergency hospital, and anyone who needs further treatment, they have to fly him or drive him up to Darwin. I spent eighteen days continuously in Darwin, between hospitals, and surgery and biopsy. During those eighteen days, I had a lot of different things happen to me. One of them, they call it nuclear scan. That nuclear scan was horrible. They made it especially for my heart, to see if my heart would survive with the type of chemo chemicals or not. They put me on my side in a cylinder that swung me like a baby, while they hit me with all types of rays and atomic things. I was in there for an hour and a half, in this little bowl, swinging until I felt sick.

"I couldn't eat after this scan. After this nuclear bomb. I couldn't sleep, and I felt my heart jumping out of my chest all night. And I thought, *I will not last to the morning. My heart is jump-jumping out of my chest. I cannot. I will not survive to the morning. I know that I'm dying tonight, and I don't want to die in the bed.* So, I sleep on a couch on my side, and I kept doing the prayers until I went to sleep. I opened my eyes in the morning and the pain was gone. Another chance for my life from Allah.

"The nuclear bomb results say it's confirmed. There are lots of swollen nodes in my body, but there are three main ones. The biggest one is in my guts. That is 58 millimetres. This is a big one. The second one is right next to my spine. This is 22 millimetres. And then the last one. Behind my heart. This is the one I feel I have known about. Ever since we were in Egypt, getting ready to come to Australia. That shadow behind my heart. She is 27 millimetres.

"There's two ways to treat a cancer like mine. You can wait and monitor to see if it will affect you. If it does, then you might do surgery to cut it out to try and get rid of it. The other is to hit it straightaway, with chemicals, burn it out. So you can go back to life.

"I had to have six cycles of chemotherapy in Darwin. Every three weeks I would have a cycle. Physically, the cycle would hit the body and destroy all the blood cells. All of them, good and bad. Then my body would start rebuilding a little bit. After three weeks, we hit it again. So, they hit me six times in Darwin. From eight o'clock in the morning to five o'clock in the afternoon I would sit in the chair, and they would pump this chemical into me.

"But it is not all bad, and it is not all pain. In Darwin, I would stay in a place called Barbara James House. I owe this house the most—after Allah, of course. For people with cancer who live far away from hospitals, things are expensive. Sometimes it's impossible to afford travel and accommodation to get better. But I was lucky. This was a good place. Good, clean rooms and nice hall for all your meals. While you are in the hall you see different people in different stages in their treatment, and you talk to them. They tell you about their cancer, and you tell them about yours, and you don't feel so bad. Part of my job in Katherine was to travel to remote communities to talk to people about how they feel about the construction happening around Katherine. About developments and infrastructure and facilities. When I went to Barbara James House, I saw people who looked familiar. I realised they were from the remote places I had been. People I had talked to, who I had no idea were sick too. And we were there together, sharing our stories. All in Darwin, because we had no other option.

"After three months, halfway through my six-cycle treatment, they looked inside me again to see if anything had changed. The node that was in my guts had gone from

58 millimetres to eight. The one near my spine was very small too. Only a couple of millimetres. And the one behind my heart had completely disappeared, like it was never there. And at the end of the six cycles, they say, 'Congratulations. There is no evidence for enlarged lymph nodes. You are in remission.' This is what the oncologist said to me.

"This word, remission, 1 ask if it means something. 1 know it means you are getting better, but 1 want to know if it means something else too. He said sometimes cancer can come back. Maybe after a year, or twenty years. Sometimes never. But he said to me, 'In your case, 1 can tell you, you will not die from cancer, you will die from something else.'

"That's when 1 come to the good bit. The maintenance. Six times a year, one day in the chair. And 1 chose to do this with you, Soos. Close to you, at Gold Coast Hospital. So, every couple of months, 1 fly down, and we can have something to do together."

❧ ❧ ❧ RULE NO. 23 ❧ ❧ ❧

PAY
YOUR RENT

I NEVER THOUGHT I WOULD get married in this country. Since that moment in my bedroom when my father told me I would have to marry a Muslim man, I thought it would never be practical.

This is what I want: someone I love who won't upset my father. Who understands that I do what I do because I want to make my father happy. Who understands that he does what he does because he wants to do the right thing. I think about the loss that has come with my grandfather's death. He lost out, not Mama. He died alone. Mama has us. All this time I have been afraid to disappoint my father, because I don't want him to hate me. I don't want him to cut me out of his life. I don't want to remove myself, like my mother did. But I think he feels the same. He doesn't want to be alone. He wants me to do the right thing, yet it's not always clear what that means. Especially here.

I am moving out of home. I am only moving out because I am getting married. I have stuck to this rule: no living on your own until you are married. The real estate agent is rude and doesn't talk to us at the inspection. He just unlocks the door and pulls out his phone. Aaron whispers to me that he can see him on Sportsbet.

Aaron. Xbox-or-PlayStation Aaron. Long-sleeves-at-the-gym Aaron. The boy I interviewed for school captain seven years ago. Aaron and I have been orbiting around each other since we were ten years old. We went to the same primary school, the same high school. We had friends in the same circles. But for the longest time I didn't speak to him—we always seemed one step removed. But now we're coming together. Becoming parts of each other.

There are four other couples inspecting the same house. None of them take off their shoes when they enter. It is a wet day, and they track mud onto the carpet. The carpet hasn't been cleaned, I can see that, but I wonder, why make it worse?

We are often made to feel like visitors in this country. One slip and we're done. We are careful not to track in mud. We take our shoes off before we go inside. That's part of what we believe in. That's part of Sharia. When you're in a country, you obey the laws of that country. Just like when you're in a rental, you don't mark the walls. But people still see us as muddy. They keep us out. If they don't, you feel they want to.

I am from no one place, like my mother. As I get older, I am realising that maybe that's the easiest way. I am not from there, and I am not from here. Maybe it's easier to come with no history, with no story, no set of rules to follow. I am my own person, I tell myself, I can pick and choose my own rules. But it's hard without a blueprint.

I am in a borrowed body, my father says, one that will be returned to Allah. I have to keep it proper. But right now, as I see it, it belongs to me. I am in control. Maybe I won't get my bond back, but I want to be happy. That counts, doesn't it? That I am happy here and now. We can think about the after when it comes.

We take our shoes off before we step into a house. Aaron knows this, and he copies me. He walks behind me, in my steps.

Aaron didn't become a school captain, but he went on to be an English mentor. He is unassuming and he is kind. He is the most reliable person I have met in my life. He has always been there. He listens to me, and he understands. Or at least, he tries to understand. There are things he will never grasp, and I think we both accept that. He proposed to me on my birthday, when no one was around. Only then did he meet my father. Baba says this was not the right way to do things, the correct sequence, but there was no other way for us. Baba says Aaron's Arabic name is Haroon. Haroon was Moses's younger brother. It's a holy name. He likes that.

My father is excited for me, and I know the rules. I have to marry a Muslim. I think of the girl I saw in the mosque that day. It seems like that is the only way for us.

Mohamed and Emma have been together for almost a decade and are not married. But that doesn't bother my father right now, because he's concerned with us, me and Aaron. I can't imagine my life without Aaron.

It is raining outside and the puddles are forming on the front lawn. Sometimes a sunny day makes it easier to sell a house. But we are not buying. We are only here to borrow.

When Aaron officially became Haroon, he accepted what came with that. Part of me wishes he didn't have to, but he did it anyway. We haven't had a wedding yet, not a big white Australian one, but we are married in the eyes of God.

On the day we move in, the house smells of paint, and the sun streams in through the back window. A kid next door is practising tuba. Maybe this is my karma—my trade with Allah for putting my parents through all that pain for all those years. I will never allow my children to play the baritone, legacy be damned.

We do not have a salon in this house. We do not have furniture trimmed in gold. We do not have a lot of things. But we have peace. And we have a picture of us. We cannot hang it on the wall, because we are not allowed to make holes. But we place it on a shelf, where it gets some light.

I look outside and say, "It's a little muddy out there."

Aaron doesn't see the ground from where he is standing. "It looks sunny to me," he says.

ACKNOWLEDGEMENTS

MUDDY PEOPLE IS BASED ON memories of my childhood. These are often fragmentary and fallible, as memories tend to be. This is a work of creative non-fiction—not a factual or verbatim recount of events and conversations. In some instances, I have streamlined the narrative to avoid unloading too much information on readers, as well as to protect the identities of the people involved. I have changed the names of several people and places mentioned. I have chosen to construct Carly, Tamara, Jason and the teachers mentioned in the story as composite characters; the actions of these characters cannot be attributed to one person alone.

Thank you endlessly to my family, for your good humour and willingness to share parts of yourselves in these pages. To my parents, for creating and being my world. This book, and everything I do, is for you. To Nana, for all you've taught me. To Aisha, for being my first and favourite reader. To Mohamed, I will give you fifty bucks if you've read this far. To Aaron, for bearing the brunt of my book-writing mood swings. Bless you.

This book was written as part of my Master of Fine Arts project. Thanks goes to my thesis supervisor, Rohan Wilson, for his steadfast support, and for being a helpful ear to my chatter. To my dear friends Alex Philp, Tess Brooks and Bizzi Lavelle, for your eyes, minds and hearts as you read an early version of this book. To Maxine Beneba Clarke, Randa Abdel-Fattah and Sara Saleh for being champions and inspirations, and for seeing something in me and my work in those early days. To Michael Mohammed Ahmad, Mona Eltahawy and Alice Pung for embracing this book. I am warmed by your support. I cannot thank you all enough.

I owe a lot to my editor, Julia Carlomagno, for her kindness, understanding, diligence and heart. Julia, you are a legend. I am so proud of what we have created together. Thank you to Sophy Williams, for our chat that fateful day at Byron Writers Festival, Thank you Sallie Butler, Erin Sandiford, and Jess McMillan from Black Inc., and to the team at Greystone Books, for all of your hard work in sharing this book with the world.

In writing this memoir I am able to share my story; I am able to speak and be heard. In a world where voices of Arabs are often relegated, censored and silenced, this is sadly a privilege. As I write these final words, in 2021, the stories of Arabs continue to be erased. Lives are being lost. Memories and legacies are being destroyed. I extend my solidarity—now and forever—to the people of Palestine, who are fighting every day for their survival, their land and their freedom. Their stories need to be heard. Royalties I receive from the sale of the Australian edition of this book will be donated to Palestinian causes.